WOMEN'S SUFFRAGE IN
SCOTLAND

This book is dedicated to my husband Kim. He has supported me throughout the compilation of the book and 'put up' with me for forty years. Thanks and love.

WOMEN'S SUFFRAGE IN
SCOTLAND

CAROLE O'CONNOR

PEN & SWORD
HISTORY

AN IMPRINT OF PEN & SWORD BOOKS LTD.
YORKSHIRE – PHILADELPHIA

First published in Great Britain in 2019 by
Pen & Sword History
An imprint of
Pen & Sword Books Ltd
Yorkshire – Philadelphia

ISBN 978 1 52672 328 4

A CIP catalogue record for this book is available from the British Library.

Printed and bound in England
by TJ International Ltd, Padstow, Cornwall
Typeset in 11.5/14 point Times New Roman
by Aura Technology and Software Services, India

Pen & Sword Books Limited incorporates the imprints of Atlas,
Archaeology, Aviation, Discovery, Family History, Fiction, History,
Maritime, Military, Military Classics, Politics, Select, Transport, True
Crime, Air World, Frontline Publishing, Leo Cooper, Remember When,
Seaforth Publishing, The Praetorian Press, Wharncliffe Local History,
Wharncliffe Transport, Wharncliffe True Crime and White Owl.

For a complete list of Pen & Sword titles please contact
PEN & SWORD BOOKS LIMITED
47 Church Street, Barnsley, South Yorkshire, S70 2AS, England
E-mail: enquiries@pen-and-sword.co.uk
Website: www.pen-and-sword.co.uk

Or
PEN AND SWORD BOOKS
1950 Lawrence Rd, Havertown, PA 19083, USA
E-mail: Uspen-and-sword@casematepublishers.com
Website: www.penandswordbooks.com

Contents

Acknowledgements		vi
Foreword		vii
Introduction		x
Chapter One	Edinburgh	1
Chapter Two	Glasgow	29
Chapter Three	Dundee and Perth	45
Chapter Four	Aberdeen	63
Chapter Five	Stirling and surrounding areas	82
Chapter Six	Highlands and Islands	100
Chapter Seven	Dumfries and Galloway	116
Chapter Eight	Miscellany	127
Conclusion		137
Bibliography		140
Index		143

Acknowledgements

So many people have helped in the collaboration of this book. Some from various organisations and institutes, some people whose relatives have been suffragettes and suffragists, and also views made by three Scottish MPs.

I would like to kindly thank these people below for all their help and support, and apologies if I have missed anyone, it will just be an oversight on my part, or an addled brain! They are listed in no particular order:

Dundee Women's Trail; Stuart Gibbs; Elspeth King, Smith Museum in Stirling; Lord & Lady Aberdeen; Moira Minty; David Powell, DC Thomson & Co; Andrew Wood; Beth Sayer; Susan Kruse; Catriona & Mairhead McDougall; Graham Fraser; Fiona Jack; Glasgow Women's Library; Victoria Webb, Wellcome Collection; Gillian Murphy, LSE Library; Falkirk Community Trust; Patrick Brennan; Louise Milne; Niall & Jean Bennett; Ian Semple; Victoria Garrington, Edinburgh Museum Archives; Raymond Pratt, General Secretary SWI; Stirling Council Archives; Tessa Spence, National Records of Scotland; National Mining Museum; Mathew Jarron, University of Dundee; Sarah Pederson, Robert Gordon University of Aberdeen; Dundee Jute Museum; Scottish Parliament and politicians; *Alloa Advertiser*; National Records of Scotland; Mining Museum; Dollar Museum; National Library of Scotland; Leith Women's Institute; Historic Environmental Scotland; Dundee City Council.

Foreword

Nicola Sturgeon – First Minister for Scotland

Women's lives and experiences have undoubtedly changed over the years, both in political and non-political life. We are fortunate to be moving closer towards gender equality and towards equal representation of women in politics. But we still have a long way to go. It is important that we honour the women who came before us and who worked tirelessly for the rights we enjoy today.

Ensuring that the women of Scotland, their stories and their struggles are represented in our history books is vitally important. Women are and should always be acknowledged as an integral part of the historic record of Scotland.

Ruth Davidson – Conservative party leader for Scotland

The story of the suffragette movement is one of the most powerful in modern times. In the centenary year (2018) of the Representation of the People Act, it is important that we reflect on that struggle, all that's been achieved since and the glass ceilings that remain.

Scotland's suffragettes were an important part of the fight for women's votes. In 1906, a branch of the Women's Social and Political Union (WSPU) opened in Glasgow and three years later the formidable Flora Drummond led a march down Princes Street on horseback.

But for me, the Representation of the People Act is best characterised by its limitations. It did not, as the shorthand would have it, grant women the vote. It granted some women – and almost all men the vote.

My great-grandmother, Bessie Ritchie, would not have been among them. Despite hurdling the age barrier and raising five sons to adulthood and a daughter who died young, she did not qualify.

Because she had left school at 14 and lived in a Glasgow Corporation tenement in Tradeston, she had neither the means nor the education to be deemed worthy of political decision-making.

As a female politician, I can't help but wonder whether those enlightened souls who objected to votes for women could have imagined a time in UK politics when, simultaneously, women would hold the offices of prime minister, first minister of Scotland and first minister of Northern Ireland, plus the leaderships of Plaid Cymru, the Welsh Liberal Democrats, the Scottish Conservatives, Sinn Fein and the Alliance Party in Northern Ireland, along with the co-convenerships of the UK and Scottish Green parties.

In every part of the UK, young girls growing up can look at politics and see that women can make it to the top, and conclude so can they.

But while we have come a long way in 100 years, when it comes to parity, equality and representation, we are still not there yet. We need to look at the world of work to see that women are more likely to be paid less than men, more likely to be harassed in the workplace, less likely to be promoted, irrespective of qualifications and experience, and more likely to have their career progression hampered by having children.

So while we give thanks to those women of courage and bloody-mindedness who achieved so much in the name of suffrage, we must recommit ourselves to finishing their work. There is still much to do.

Kezia Dugdale – Member of Scottish Parliament and previous leader of Scottish Labour

The campaign theme for International Women's Day in 2017 was 'be bold for a change', a challenge that resonates with women across the world today, but was undoubtedly an even greater challenge for the women who first fought for change and equality between the mid-1800s and 1950, the years examined in this book.

Although I am extremely proud of the work that has been done to deliver gender equality over the generations, I am still outraged that today the unfortunate reality of life for women worldwide is that men continue to be paid more, on average, than a woman doing the exact same job. This is something you would believe was the norm back then, but not now.

Looking back, remembering and celebrating the proud history of women fighting for equality that this book provides is important, but it also provides an opportunity on debating what more needs to be done.

I am also a founding member of Women 50/50, which fights for at least fifty per cent representation of women in our parliament, in our councils and on public boards. Today, despite making up fifty-two per cent of the population, in Scotland women only make up thirty-six per cent of public boards, less than thirty-five per cent of MSPs (Member of the Scottish Parliament) and twenty-four per cent of councillors. It is not good enough, and it is estimated that unless radical change is pursued, it would take another fifty years for us to reach an equal parliament.

Only by reflecting on our past, can we focus on our future. This book will provide a valuable insight into the lives of women in Scotland at the turn of the twentieth century and explore what life for women was like then, and the road towards equality that we are still travelling on.

The 7th Marquess of Aberdeen and Temair

I am delighted to write a foreword to this book. My grandmother, Ishbel Aberdeen, was a remarkable lady, and throughout her long life she championed many worthy causes, especially for women. Denied further education herself due to the era in which she was born, she formed the Haddo House Association to further the education of girls and young women in the north-east of Scotland. She adopted the motto: Onwards and Upwards.

As she and her husband achieved high office abroad, she extended her work in both education and healthcare to a wider audience, becoming the founding president of the Victorian Order of Nurses.

Her pioneering work continued from the 1870s right up to her death in 1939, a period spanning sixty years, and my family are very proud of her achievements.

Introduction

This book is different.

Books on women's suffrage before have covered this event in history by condensing chapters into time-spans.

This current book on Scottish suffragettes/suffragists aims to examine the various areas of Scotland, such as large towns and cities (with information where possible on surrounding areas).

Research will view in each chapter the impact of women's daily lives throughout history leading up to and after the suffrage movement.

Each individual area/s will document through these different times, and we will see how Scottish women were treated, fairly or otherwise, when it came to work, education, daily life and, of course, voting.

To gain insight into these Scottish areas, some detail will be given at the start of each chapter on a brief history of that region. Subheadings such as health, work, education, leisure and family life will show the impact on Scottish women's everyday lives and how, for many, the fight for survival to remain well and to be heard and seen as equals and not the home-makers many felt they should be.

Is this book not about women's suffrage in Scotland? Yes it is, but women's day-to-day existence, pre- and post- the 1918 vote for women, shows how these women endured various situations to provide for their families. Perhaps their feelings of worth and equality, and voicing their opinions were slowly building.

Suffrage is all about the right to vote. Looking back into parliament and its history, it would appear Scottish women were, on the whole, good home-makers and jobs as domestic servants and quite often textile workers were dominant job roles in those earlier periods.

Even as far back as the late 1500s it was definitely a man's world. When a woman married it was written that: 'a wife is in subjection and under governance of her husband, as long as they both continue alive.' This was often written into the marriage service.

As this book focuses on women's suffrage, that is the main objective. However, it must not be forgotten about men's sympathies for women's plight. There were groups such as the Northern Men's Federation for Women's Suffrage and many others who supported women.

It is fair to say men have not had easy times either. Women were not conscripted in the First World War, as were their menfolk, but some females took on the roles left by men as they went to war. Thousands of women assisted the military in support roles such as nursing, driving ambulances and working in intelligence. At home they worked in munitions factories, on the railways, in the police, and as bus drivers and bus conductors, to name just a few. Women played important roles in history, but still could not vote before 1918, and only then if they were over 30.

The first mention of women's suffrage appears to be about 1817, by Jeremy Bentham. Born in London in 1748, he trained as a lawyer but never practised. He focused on injustice and wrote several books. He published *A plan of parliamentary reform in the form of catechism.* He spoke up for equality of women and chose to be a reformist early on in his life. It is said he found 'the placing of women in legally inferior positions' unacceptable. There follows a brief look at the roots of Scottish parliament and how things have changed over the years regarding voting in in general. A timeline below offers an outline of Reform Acts, sometimes known as Representation of the People Acts, and a failed Bill, showing what had changed during those periods:

Various UK parliamentary Acts/Bills affecting voting

DATE	REFORM ACT	EFFECT
1832	First Reform Act	Over 650,000 people could vote, no secret voting. Adult male householders in boroughs could vote. Majority of working men and all women could NOT vote

DATE	REFORM ACT	EFFECT
1867	Second Reform Act	Working-class householders aged 21, in cities got the vote, countryside householders got vote in 1884. Non-householders not until 1918 and still NO VOTES FOR WOMEN
1872	Secret Ballot Act	Introduction of secret ballot
1883	Corrupt Practices Act	Candidates were allotted campaign times
1884	Third Reform Act	Two out of three men now had the vote. Counties were given same political rights as boroughs. Eighteen per cent of male population now voted. NO VOTES FOR WOMEN
1885	Redistribution of Seats Act	Scotland was given another twelve seats. Constituencies were reorganised. Two MPs for town populations 50,000-165,000
1910	Conciliation Bill	Bill written to extend voting rights to women. But it failed to become law
1913	'Cat & Mouse Act' The Prisoners Temporary Discharge for Ill Health Act	Women who had been imprisoned were temporarily released if they were in ill health, but returned to prison once better
1918	Representation of the People Act 1918	Women over 30 were allowed to vote, and men over 21
1928	Representation of the People Act 1928	Women now had equal franchise with men. Voting was age 21 and for both sexes

A simple and brief explanation of the beginnings of Scottish parliament may help to understand how and why it all started and where, if at any time, Scottish women featured in parliament and voting, in any shape or form.

According to the current Scottish parliament website, here is a brief breakdown of historical politics:

Scottish parliament – a brief historical outlook

(information used from Scottish parliament timeline)

YEAR	WHAT IT WAS
1235	A meeting at Kirkliston, Edinburgh, is the first identifiable parliament in Scotland. Nobles and clergy advised King Alexander II on justice
1293	King John Balliol was head of parliamentary meetings. It appears he dealt with a great deal of land/tenement disputes
1309	King Robert Bruce is supported at St Andrews parliament by the clergy
1357	King David's parliament consisted of '3 estates'. These were clergy, knights and 'burghs'(town) council members. Taxes, legislation, justice were some items they dealt with
1424-1426	James I at Perth parliament attempted to change ways of parliament, similar to that in England, but he failed
1437-1460	James II promised not to change legislation. Unrest in parliament
1471	James III and parliament believed football (futeball) and golf distracted folk from work and were therefore banned. Women worth less than £100 were not allowed to wear silk as a lining, only on collars and sleeves
1496	Education Act allowed only sons of wealthy landowners and barons schooling
1532	James V at Edinburgh parliament set up court of session. The king wanted a permanent order of justice for the well-being of everyone
1560	Reformation of parliament. Protestant religion set up, and ties broken with the pope and Catholic faith. Parliament sealed the deal
1563	Queen Mary I at Edinburgh parliament, persuaded by the church to pass the Witchcraft Act. Hundreds of witches (or maybe healers) were put to death

YEAR	WHAT IT WAS
1579	James V reigns. Poor Law Act enforced to help those living in poverty. However, if they could, but wouldn't work, they were put in the stocks, children taken away, and girls up to 18, and boys up until 24 were sent into service
1604	James VI now reigns, and proposed parliamentary union with England, which failed
1634	Parliament House built in Edinburgh
1642	Scottish parliament was abolished but allowed to bring representatives to Westminster. Oliver Cromwell occupies Scotland
1661	King Charles II reigns, Scottish parliament restored
1707	Union of Scotland with England, all to sit in parliament in Westminster
1832 & 1867	Both reform Acts gave more people the vote. But not women
1892	Scotland's **Keir Hardie** elected as MP for West Ham
1918	Votes for women over 30
1928	Votes for women over 21
1939	Functions of the Scottish government moved from London to Edinburgh
1979	A 'yes' referendum had 77,000 votes but only accounted for 32.9% of electorate
1997	People of Scotland voted on a devolved Scottish parliament with tax varying powers
1999	First Scottish parliament elections. Coalition of Labour and Liberals
2003	Second Scottish parliament elections. Coalition as above
2004	New parliament building near Holyrood opened by the queen
2007	Third Scottish parliament elections. Scottish National Party (SNP) in power
2011	Fourth Scottish parliament elections. As above

Influential men at the beginning of the campaign for women's suffrage included John Stuart Mill MP, Jacob Bright and Keir Hardie MP. In 1866, John Mill MP (Liberal) was the first male to call for votes for women. He said that the inequality of women was a relic from the past, when 'might was right.' In 1867, he requested that 'man' be changed to 'person' in the Representation of the People Act, which failed with only a third of parliament backing him.

In 1868, women ratepayers were allowed to vote on elections for school boards, town and county councils, and poor law boards, in the updated Reform Act. This had a knock-on effect on demands for further education and professions for women, which eventually happened in 1892.

Although much has been documented about suffrage consisting mainly of middle-class women, many working-class females also supported the movement. It is fair to say that the latter were often involved in standing up for rights such as patronage riots, meal mobs, work riots due to poor working conditions, unfair pay, and so on.

It is often said that between 1885 and 1905, the suffrage movement, although still around, was not at the forefront of political debates. However, many petitions and various MPs, such as William Woodall in 1884 and Sir Albert Rollit in 1892, tried in vain to gain enfranchisement for women. Mr Faithfull Begg, MP for Glasgow, finally in 1897 had his second reading of the Reform Bill favoured by seventy-one votes. He was parliamentary advisor to the National Union of Suffrage Societies.

So many people were involved in UK women's suffrage, both in England and Scotland. From Mary Wollstonecraft's book in 1792, *Vindication of the Rights of Woman,* Marion Kirkland Reid's book in 1843, *A Plea for a Woman,* and the first petition in 1832 to Westminster, by a Yorkshire lady, Mary Smith, to MP John Mill's call for an amendment to the Reform Act 1867, the Pankhursts, Emmeline and daughters, Christabel, Adela and Sylvia, and the list goes on. The year 2018 was the centenary of women's enfranchisement, and both Scottish and British parliaments responded to the hundredth anniversary with talks, lectures, tea parties and exhibitions in the

Vote 100 project. Scottish first minister Nicola Sturgeon actively encouraged more women into politics by granting £500,000 to help this cause. At present, only a third of MSPs are women.

Women are moving up to higher positions in professions, but still slowly. Engender, the feminist organisation, stated in a recent study that only twenty-seven per cent of women held Scottish leadership roles.

It may take more time and more energy, but what those early suffragettes and suffragists did for women and votes has set the scene for then, now and years to come for females to surge forward and be counted.

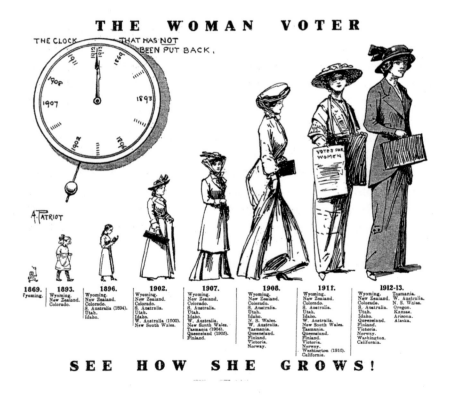

Votes for Women, 13 June, 1913

Women voter poster. (Courtesy of city of Edinburgh Museums and Galleries)

CHAPTER ONE

Edinburgh

Brief history

The city itself can be traced back to the Middle Ages, but a new town was formed in the eighteenth century.

Edinburgh lies in the central area of Scotland. The main river that flows through the area is the Water of Leith. Edinburgh Castle peers down from Castle Rock over the southerly aspect of the city. There has been a castle here since the twelfth century. However, in the eighteenth century the vaults were used to house prisoners, but after forty-nine escaped in 1811, this ceased and the castle became a monument. Visitors were admitted from the 1830s.

As with most areas in England and Scotland, Edinburgh had poor sanitary and living conditions in the eighteenth century. Writer and journalist Daniel Defoe wrote in his book in the 1700s, *A tour thro' the whole island of Great Britain*, 'In no city in the world, so many people live in so little room as Edinburgh.' Cholera was rife in the 1800s due to the bad sanitation and overcrowding. When the new town was built, professional people moved to the area from the old town.

Briefly, in Edinburgh the population was:

1755 = 57,195
1791 = 81,865
1811 = 103,143 (44,290 males, 58,853 females)
1841 = 133,692 (58,642 males, 75,050 females)
1891 = 269.407 (122,921 males, 146,486 females)
1911 = 436,456 (200,185 males, 236,271 females)
1931 = 438,297 (199,460 males, 238,837 females)
1991 = 415,968 (185,193 males, 220,775 females)

2011 = 476,626 (232,364 males, 244,262 females)
2015 = 498,800 (243,000 males, 256,000 females) (to the nearest thousand)

Through the years it is easy to see that females dominated the population in figures.

Holyrood Palace (built on abbey grounds in 1501 by James IV and transformed into a more substantial palace in 1670), Edinburgh Castle (twelfth century), and Edinburgh University (opened in the late 1500s) are all famous landmarks in Edinburgh history.

At the palace and the castle women were employed as maids, servants and kitchen staff, and in the castle there would have been a housekeeper and domestic staff. These types of jobs were desirable to a lot of folk due to the prestige, even if the wages were not high.

The university, which opened in 1583, was not without its prejudices regarding allowing women into its premises to study. The first female graduates were finally allowed in 1893, of which there were eight. This was thanks to the Universities (Scotland) Act 1889.

Working life

In Edinburgh, the biggest percentage of working women were again in the domestic services, with a total of seventy per cent of the female workforce engaged in this employment. This was followed by twenty-three per cent working in industry. As with most Scottish cities, textiles were an important and flourishing employment in this era. The Bank of Scotland opened its head office just outside Edinburgh in 1783. It was not until the First World War in 1914 that the bank actually employed larger numbers of female workers to fill the gap while the men were at war. Previously, bank work was considered a male-only environment. It appears in London a handful of women were taken on as female typists, but there were strict rules, such as not talking to the male colleagues on stairs or in passageways. Even in the 1920s, female bank employees had to be between the ages of 17 and 30 and unmarried. Once they were married they had to resign.

Edinburgh was the legal and financial centre in Scotland, but domestic service and textile industry was still the dominant employment for women in the 1800s.

Some females were able to run shops, but The Merchant Company of Edinburgh stated (about female shopkeepers): 'they have no title to the privilege of trade in this city, which is hurtful to the trading burgesses, who bear the public burdens of the place.'

Both men and women had to pay entry fees or buy licences to trade through this company. Some women traded through family members, and it is also thought that, as the Merchant Company was low on funds, women therefore boosted their finances.

These women fought to obtain decent employment and education, which in turn led to them fighting for their right to vote.

As early as 1735, it was noted that the wife of Robert Cummings, Deacon of Edinburgh Fletchers, had dealt with his affairs.

A paper mill in Penicuik (midway between Edinburgh and Peebles) declared in the mid-1800s that in order to prevent the neglect of children in their homes, it did not employ mothers of young children, the exception being widows or those whose husbands could not earn a living.

In Edinburgh in the nineteenth century, domestic work for women, which was originally one of the four major employment areas including textiles, clothing and agriculture, switched towards industry. Prior to 1871, more than ninety per cent of women worked in those areas. But employment in the city for females was overtaken by working in industries such as bookbinding and food processing. Domestic service fell from seventy per cent in 1841 to just forty per cent in 1914.

The teaching profession was a particularly hard area for women once they were married. A marriage bar was in place in many Scottish areas (apart from Dundee), stating once wed they had to give up their profession. This outdated policy remained until the 1950s.

During the First World War, a great deal changed for women. They worked in engineering workshops to produce armaments and in shipyards and, as previously mentioned, they were employed on trams and buses. Many worked as conductors. However, this was short-lived. When the war was over, the jobs they had been employed to do, on the whole, were given back to the men returning from war.

Shop work was another area where women flourished. One account from Peggy Watson (*Edinburgh Memories*) stated she was paid 2 shillings per week (about 10 pence in today's money), working in a general store.

Jenners department store in Princes Street opened in 1892 but burned down in 1893. It was rebuilt in 1895. As with many department stores springing up in the UK from the 1860s, many women were employed as shop girls. Half of the employees in these stores were women.

The architecture on the front of the Jenners building shows many female characters, depicting the support women gave by shopping in the store. It was noted that women shoppers could shop unaccompanied without damaging their reputation.

Jenners was the only store to provide accommodation for its staff (male and female). At the time there was a demand for young females working away to be supervised, and it would seem providing a roof over their heads was a good idea. It appears that many local girls were employed, but also refined young ladies of good breeding, some from as far away as England, came to work at Jenners.

Clerical work, retail work and professions such as nursing and midwifery provided women with employment. However, training to be a doctor proved more difficult.

Holyrood Palace offered desirable employment. Pay for women was not generous, but working for a royal household, the belief was often you could be singled out as a favourite.

The hours would have been long, and quite often the maids of honour had a great deal of waiting and watching, wore heavy uniforms, there was no privacy, and while on duty they were not allowed to sit. This was the price to pay for working in a prestigious environment.

Health & welfare

Overcrowding in cities such as Edinburgh was common among the poor. Sometimes as many as twelve to sixteen people, including children, occupied a room in the poorer areas. This in turn led to higher death rates.

In 1860, in Tron, the death rate was 353 persons per acre, Canongate was 238 persons per acre and Grassmarket 220 persons per acre. Deaths were usually due to typhus, tuberculosis (TB), whooping cough, smallpox, measles and scarlatina. Most of these diseases are now preventable and were airborne-spread. Typhus was caused by fleas (lice) spreading from one person to another. However, cholera and typhoid, which were caused by raw sewage found in drinking water, also accounted for many deaths. Overcrowding, poor hygiene and people living in close proximity to each other did not help the situation.

When Glasgow extracted water from Loch Katrine in 1855, Edinburgh and other cities followed, and the diseases and deaths were reduced dramatically, due to the improved water supplies.

Just before the 1800s, a Magadalen Asylum was established in Edinburgh. It was home to prostitutes, single mums and socialists. Its aim was to 'cleanse morals and rehabilitate fallen women'.

It is estimated that in the 1800s there were over 200 brothels in Edinburgh, and some girls were only aged 9 and 10. Times were hard and there is no denying many of these women and young girls were forced to turn to this trade in order to survive, eat and bring money into whatever home they lived in.

In 1871, a census showed that a Clyde street brothel run by a Clara Johnson, the 'gay girls' as she named them, could earn more than the small amount of £8 per year their respectable jobs paid them.

Unfortunately, research shows that often a great deal of these women did not live past the age of 30. Their lives were overtaken by brutality and disease.

In a book entitled *Rangers – Ladies of Pleasure in Edinburgh*, dated 1775, there was even mention of a lady whose father was a wealthy baronet, herself having financial problems, becoming a 'loose woman'. However, in a 2017 article by a distant relative, on a blog for the National Library of Scotland, it was suggested that this was probably a false accusation. Whatever the truth, it is sad to discover that so many women resorted to this trade too often just to make ends meet.

The National Insurance Act 1911 helped the male folk with health care, but not the women or children. It was argued the man was the main breadwinner, and it was better to get him back to health.

In 1868 there were more than fifty poorhouses in Glasgow and Edinburgh. Women often gave birth at home as they couldn't afford to go to hospital. To engage a doctor in the early 1900s there was a charge of 3s 6d (17½ pence), which was a great deal of money.

Of course, times were hard for all the family, but women could not afford to be ill, with the home to run, children to look after and many females working in between to supplement the male wages.

The National Health Service commenced in 1948, celebrating seventy years in 2018. This then provided free health care for the UK population. Edinburgh, however, in 1913, had directly run a state-funded health system entitled Highlands and Islands Medical Service, covering some of the crofting areas. It was not a free service, but only small fees were observed and if the poor could not pay, they were still treated.

Public baths and washhouses were installed in Edinburgh in 1880, to help with poor hygiene and the lack of washing facilities which in turn had led to diseases and sometimes death. Six buildings were erected around the city. Women could take their clothes and linens to wash and also wash themselves and children. Often, they would take washing along that others were unable to do. Sometimes they were paid and sometimes they did it out of kindness. To use the washhouses there were charges and these were reported as being higher in Scotland than in England. Some of the Edinburgh washhouses were not well ventilated, causing fumes from the engine room. And natural light was often poor. But it was the first step towards alleviating some of the health problems in the city.

It is necessary to build a picture of what life was like for Edinburgh women, and indeed Scottish women, throughout history (predominantly the eighteenth century onwards for this book). Their hard work and determination throughout the years led towards to the vote for women and equality (for the most part) for women.

Education

Education for poorer girls in the eighteenth century was predominantly by dame schools. Possibly a teacher was in place, but more often local women taught the young girls to read, sew and cook. Only a few could write and count.

An important fact to note was even as far back as the sixteenth century females were believed in the main to have little intellect compared to the males, and thus had some education but not on the same scale as boys. About ninety per cent of female servants in the seventeenth and eighteenth centuries were illiterate.

Noble females undoubtedly were better educated, one example being Mary Queen of Scots.

In Edinburgh in the early 1800s, school mistresses only taught younger children and older girls, but not in parish schools, only private establishments. Male teachers (dominies) taught the boys.

The 1872 Education (Scotland) Act's aim was for more children to go to school, making it compulsory for all children aged 5-13 to attend. School boards now looked after more than 500 parish schools that were originally run by the church. Not all children could be reached, but there was still discrimination against female teachers. Although there were more women teachers than men, women were regarded as inferior and the pay they received was far less than the male teachers!

School masters and mistresses originally did not receive adequate training. But in the mid-1800s, Market Street Sessional School commenced proper teaching training qualifications.

Reverend Thomas Guthrie, appalled at the lack of education for some children, opened a Ragged School. Girls of 1847 could learn the 3Rs (reading, writing and arithmetic) and be accommodated at the school. In 1875, in Lovers Lane, Leith Walk, Edinburgh, there were at least eighty girls at the premises aged between 7 and 12. According to the 1881 census, there was one young matron, one teacher and two servants who undertook cooking and cleaning. All were female.

In 1890, school fees were abolished, and state-funding was given for schools.

The Royal High School on Regent Road, Edinburgh, is believed to be the oldest school in the world, dating back to around 1128. It appears to have originally been a fee-paying school for boys, but girls were eventually admitted, possibly in 1968 when the school became co-educational and moved from Regent Road to its current position in Barton.

The 1918 Education Act deemed free secondary education for children, which saw a major growth for girls.

Another school in Edinburgh is the James Gillespie School. The said Mr Gillespie was a wealthy tobacco merchant who, on his death in the late 1700s, bequeathed his estate as a poor hospital and a school for poor boys. However, by the mid-twentieth century, it had become a high school for girls, and in 1975 the school became a state comprehensive school with the primary teaching aspect separated to become its own unit.

Edinburgh author Dame Muriel Spark was a pupil at the school (1923-1935) and it is alleged that her famous novel. *The Prime of Miss Jean Brodie* was based on one of her teachers there.

In Edinburgh in the early nineteenth century, some old residential hospitals were changed into fee-paying schools for the middle classes, and hence working-class parents could not afford to send their children there. Girls from aristocratic families fared better with subjects covering literacy, numeracy, cooking, sewing, household management and manners. These girls were usually taught at home by a governess or tutor.

In Scotland as a whole in 1851, sixty-five per cent of teachers were male. But by 1911, seventy per cent were female. Male teachers were paid £121-£143 per year compared to female teachers who only received £62-£72 per year. It was argued at the time that the women did not hold the same teaching qualifications as their male counterparts. However, after 1905, more female teachers sought proper qualifications. From 1914, the figure for certified women teachers rose to sixty-five per cent and they, therefore, sought to claim equal pay. Men claimed that women were not the main breadwinners, so this would be unfair. It appears it wasn't until 1962 that teacher pay scales for women caught up with the men.

There has been argument in recent years according to Insight (a research group with SEED/Secondary Education to Encourage Development) that there are fewer male teachers in the profession, causing the loss of male role for male pupils.

As time has passed with education it is clear that opportunities for females have improved for secondary education, certainly from when the Labour government in 1965 made all comprehensive schools non-selective.

Suffrage, politics, women and notable men

The Edinburgh Female Anti-Slavery Society and the Edinburgh Emancipation Society are just two groups in the early 1800s that saw women campaign against slavery. They would boycott slave-grown products, and it would seem the women gained progress in the form of 'outside the box' politics.

Quaker Eliza Smeal Wigham attempted to move the Edinburgh society on an independent course for women's rights from the emancipation society. Many of the abolitionists were from middle class backgrounds, but it also clear that working- and lower-class women also joined the societies.

William Gladstone was prime minister in 1884 when the Third Reform Act gave more enfranchisement to men. Women were still ignored in gaining the vote. Despite the setback again, the Ladies Edinburgh Debating Society asked: 'Is the enfranchisement of women desirable?' The result was a majority decision by five of YES.

In April 1892, Gladstone wrote a letter to Sam Smith MP, stating reasons for not giving women the vote. In his closing paragraph he said:

> I admit in the universities, professions, and secondary circles of public action, we have already given a shadow of plausibility to the present proposals to go farther, but it is only a shadow, we have done nothing that plunges women into the turmoil of masculine life. My disposition is to do all that is free from danger and reproach but take no further step until I am convinced of its safety. The affirmation pleas are not clear to my mind.
>
> I honestly hope that the House of Commons will decline the second reading of the Women's Suffrage Bill.

It would seem he felt women couldn't deal with the vote and he was protecting them. Or was he worried that females may have gone on to take parliamentary roles? What would he think about today's parliament?

It was noted at a meeting in Edinburgh's National Women's Suffrage in late 1886 how far women had actually progressed regarding positions such as sitting on school boards, voting in church on relevant matters, and taking up other public positions. These were all noted by Millicent Garrett Fawcett (a British suffragist, 1847-1929), who spoke of this following a discussion with a 90-year-old Scottish woman who had witnessed these changes. In April 2018, a statue of Millicent was erected in Parliament Square.

The Primrose League (1883) was another organisation, based on Conservative ideals, that had a ladies branch, one in Edinburgh. It has been said this was the first political organisation that gave women the same status and responsibilities as men. In the 1880s, the grand council of the Primrose League did not wish to delve into the suggestion of women's franchise. Indeed, they had many female members who did not want the vote, but were happy to do 'their bit' for the League.

In Edinburgh in January 1887, according to *Women's Suffrage Journal*, an Edinburgh solicitor had spoken the previous month at a Primrose League meeting at the Scott Habitation (lodges where they met). He spoke about giving enfranchisement to unmarried

WHERE WOMEN VOTE—
THERE IS NO REST

Anti suffrage postcard.
(Courtesy of LSE
Library)

females holding property qualifications, and the motion was
enthusiastically carried to a majority.

Catherine Blair was a farmer's daughter born in 1872 in East
Lothian. She was a suffragette but also instrumental in forming
the Scottish Women's Rural Institute, the first being in 1917 in
Longniddry (12 miles east of Edinburgh).

Her mother died when she was young, so her aunt brought her
and her siblings up, after marrying their father.

Catherine said in a letter to a Mrs Ratcliffe concerning her
forthcoming *Rural Institute* book in 1940 that a distant kinsman,
Sir James Young Simpson, a chloroformist, was criticised angrily

by the ministers of the day for using chloroform during childbirth, because he was 'taking away the curse from women'. Catherine went on to say this was what made her an ardent suffragette. This lady did not take part in any militant action, but she did write many letters to the papers putting arguments forward for the franchise of women and often pointing out to the press the inconsistency of their articles. She continued in her letter, saying the suffragettes she gave refuge to laughed when they read in the newspapers that they were supposed to have escaped to France.

Catherine spoke at many meetings, and some of the early Women's Institute (WI) syllabus included talks on genial subjects such as cooking and crafts, but also on debatable items such as 'Our position and powers as voters' and 'Does the state do too much or too little for us'.

Of course, not every woman was interested in the vote. When Catherine was trying to involve women in the Institute meeting, many farming females had never attended public meetings, let alone considered enfranchisement, as they were too busy on their farms. At the time, just before the First World War, Catherine recalled one farmer's wife saying: 'I have a good husband and home, and

Catherine Blair (second from left). (Courtesy of her great granddaughters)

I don't want a vote.' Today there survive three scrapbooks, owned by Catherine's great-granddaughters, Catriona and Mairead. They contain many cuttings of letters and thoughts by Catherine on the suffragette movement.

It is interesting to note that in Catherine's scrapbook about the Women's Conference for Peace in 1915 is a cutting from English suffragist Mrs Pethwick Lawrence, of a letter penned by her to a newspaper. It stated the British government had refused her a passport to travel. She did, in the end, attend the event and she spoke about women's enfranchisement.

Nannie (Agnes) Brown was born in Princes Street, Edinburgh, in 1866. She and her sister **Jessie** were active members of the 1909 Women's Freedom League (WFL) in Edinburgh, which favoured passive resistance and civil disobedience. But they did not support the sometimes violent actions by the WSPU.

In 1912, she and five other women marched from Edinburgh to London in support of women's suffrage. It took them five weeks, but *en route* they held open-air meetings and gathered signatures in a bid to present Prime Minister Asquith with the petition. Nannie Brown was presented with a silver badge for walking the 400-plus miles to London.

Nannie and Jessie were known to heckle parliamentary candidates and speak at meetings, but Nannie was also a writer of stories, lectures, plays and articles. She was heavily involved, in 1917, with the Scottish Women's Rural Institute (SWRI), alongside Catherine Blair, often holding healthy debates with her on the society of the times.

Another involvement for Nannie was as one of the founder members of the Scottish Council of Women's Citizens Association. The aim of this group in 1918/19 was to encourage women's involvement in public affairs. Women over 30 now had the vote in the UK.

Some of the topics discussed at their meetings were: women in industry, women in the state, women in education and women in the home.

Nannie Brown.
(Courtesy of city
of Edinburgh
Museums and
Galleries)

As she became older and less able, Nannie's home in Castle Terrace, Edinburgh, became a haven for some of the SWRI members, where they could go for advice and support.

Sophia Jex-Blake (1840-1912). Although a feminist and born in England, mention must be given to this remarkable woman who eventually, through strong opposition, became the first female doctor in Scotland. She trained at Edinburgh University at the age of 29 and was initially refused on the grounds the university could not 'make necessary arrangements in the interest of one lady'.

Unperturbed, she advertised in the *Scotsman* and other newspapers. Six other females joined her in fighting the cause to train as doctors and they became known as the Edinburgh Seven.

Sophia originally trained as a teacher but, when visiting the USA in 1865, she met up with Dr Lucy Sewell, a resident physician at a women and children's hospital. She found through observation that she was inspired by medicine and the need to help poorer females, who she felt were not comfortable with male doctors dealing with some of their problems.

She applied the following year at the Harvard Medical School, but was turned down. According to them the 'university did not have the provision for education of women at the university'. However, she enlisted on a training course at the New York Infirmary a few years later, but eventually had to leave due to family commitments.

Despite the prejudices in England, Sophia managed to secure a place with the other six women in 1869 at Edinburgh University, although they were taught separately from the men and their fees to study were double those of their male counterparts. A small step in the right direction it would seem, but more opposition reared its head.

Several senior male medical practitioners strongly opposed the women studying. The queen's surgeon, Professor Robert Christison, said:

> While women should be midwives, they are unsuitable material for doctoring.

One doctor, Henry Bennett, was so incensed with women studying to become doctors he said:

> What right have women to claim equality with men?

He felt women had no supreme power in the development of the sciences and only men had achieved this power.

The women were bullied and harassed over the years. In 1870, they attempted to sit their examinations and had university gates slammed in their faces by bolshy male counterparts. However, between Berne, Switzerland and Dublin, Sophia passed all her examinations and finally qualified as a doctor in 1877 and opened the Edinburgh School of Medicine for Women (ESMW) the same year.

As well as being a female doctor, Sophia wrote several books and became involved in political activities, including canvassing and organising suffrage meetings.

It is interesting to note that another student of Ms Jex-Blake's school of medicine was Elsie Maud Inglis, who studied for three years at Sophia's Edinburgh establishment. But the two did 'fall out' and Elsie opened her own medical school.

Elsie Maud Inglis (1864-1917) moved to Edinburgh at the age of 14. She was originally born in India. It is said Elsie's parents felt her education was as important as that of her brother, John, so she was privately educated. She came from a supportive family, not always the 'norm' in those early days.

At the age of 18, Elsie decided to train as a doctor and commenced her study at Sophia Jex-Blake's ESMW. However, after three years the two clashed. Elsie felt Sophia had many authoritarian ways and she believed the wrong handling of a couple of situations with other students was unacceptable. So it was that Ms Inglis opened her own medical school named the Scottish Association for the Medical Education of Women (SAMED). She went on to complete her training at Glasgow Infirmary in 1892.

Elsie had worked with people in the slum areas in Glasgow throughout her training and this seemed to spur her on the road to suffrage. She witnessed a wife being thrown out of her home by her drunken husband, and stated:

> When I have the vote I shall vote that all men who turn their wives and families out of doors, should be horsewhipped. If they make out they were tipsy, I will give them double!

A feisty woman, Elsie set out to help the position of women in society. As a newly qualified practitioner she worked at the New Hospital for Women in London coincidentally run by Elizabeth Garrett Anderson, the first British physician and surgeon and also a suffragist.

Elsie gave talks on enfranchisement while in London, but returned to Edinburgh in in 1894. She became secretary of the Scottish Federation of Women's Suffrage Societies (SFWSS) from 1906 to 1914.

As well as a day-to-day medical practitioner, it is said she spoke at least four times a week at suffrage meetings, attending meetings even as far away as the northern islands of Shetland and Orkney.

Elsie was involved with the National Union of Women's Suffrage Societies (NUWSS) with **Millicent Fawcett,** but she was opposed to the militant group for suffrage run by the Pankhursts, WSPU.

During the First World War, suffrage groups suspended their activities. In 1914, at the start of the war, Elsie volunteered her services to the Royal Army Medical Corps as a surgeon. This was turned down and she was informed by an officer to 'go home and sit still'. Likewise, the War Office rejected her volunteering.

Unperturbed, she formed the Scottish Women's Hospitals (SWH). Her services were taken up by Serbia and France, after she

Elsie Inglis.
(Courtesy of LSE
Library)

raised a great deal of money to fund hospitals, beds and medical staff. This was despite asking the Red Cross for help with funding. Head of the Red Cross, Sir George Beatson, replied 'that they could do nothing to help with a hospital staffed by women'. He claimed it was due to the organisation being under the War Office. Again, the prejudices against women seemed to have reared their ugly head, despite the conflict of war now upon the world.

Her great work in Serbia did not go unnoticed and she received The Order of the White Eagle from Crown Prince Alexander of Serbia.

Elsie died in 1917. Through leading her women's medical team to Serbia, and her efforts during the war, Elsie is believed to have thought that as women were making a valuable contribution to the war efforts, this would in turn be seen favourably. She hoped the long-awaited votes for women would soon be at the forefront.

Lady Frances Balfour (1858-1931) was the daughter of the 8th Duke of Argyll, George Douglas Campbell. Born in London she spent time in Scotland once married to Eustace Balfour, brother of the prime minister, Arthur Balfour. She lived in Ross-shire.

She was disillusioned at home. Life was not what she expected, we are led to believe. Her husband drank and her life, despite five children, was not all that happy. She found other ways in which she could channel her beliefs and thoughts. Lady Frances originally became involved with the Primrose League (interesting women in politics), the Women's Liberal Unionist Association (WLUA) and the National Council for Working Women (care of young working girls). As an aristocrat and through some of these organisations she appears to have built up networks discussing suffrage with other middle- and upper-class women. In 1896, she became president of the central committee of the National Society for Women's Suffrage.

Lady Frances did not like the militancy of suffragettes and it seems as a suffragist she was more involved in propaganda and influence. From 1910 to 1912, she recorded that she had spoken at over sixty meetings across the UK.

The *Scotsman* newspaper wrote in October 2012 that it was noted she was the highest member of the aristocracy to campaign for women's rights. In 1922, she became vice president of Edinburgh Hospital and Dispensary for Women and Children. She was also president of the Scottish Churches League for Women's Suffrage.

Lady Betty Balfour (1867-1942) was born in London and was the older sister of **Lady Constance Lytton**. Both supported the suffrage cause. However, more seems to be documented about Lady Constance than of Lady Betty. Lady Betty was also sister-in-law to Lady Frances Balfour, with whom she appears to have been close.

Lady Betty married George Balfour, youngest brother of Arthur Balfour from Lothian, Scotland, who went on to become prime minister. She joined the NUWSS and was president of the Edinburgh Conservative and Unionist Women's Franchise Association (non-militant organisation).

She and Lady Frances took it upon themselves to organise restoration for the East Lothian medieval Whitekirk Church, which was said to have been burnt down in 1914 by suffragettes. Interestingly, in 2014, it appears the local history group had a theory that it was, in fact, a lay official at the church who possibly knocked over a candle, causing the blaze and not the suffragettes, who had always vehemently denied setting fire to the church.

Lady Betty was also partly instrumental in organising a tea party in the early 1900s for her brother-in-law, Arthur Balfour, at the request of English suffragist Catherine Marshall.

According to the author Jo Vellacott, Catherine hoped for suffrage coverage by having 'someone important and that his words would be reported in all the foreign news'. Despite a *faux pas* from Catherine informing *The Times*, thus infuriating Arthur Balfour's sister, the tea party did go ahead. Arthur Balfour, Lord Lytton, Lord Robert Cecil and Arthur Steel Maitland all supported the suffragists and their campaign.

As the vote for women did not come into play until 1918, for all these politicians and gentlemen's support, it still fell short of enfranchisement for women.

Lady Constance Lytton (1869-1923). Although born in Vienna, she was heavily involved in suffrage, mainly in England. Apart from

Lady Constance
Lytton (right) with
Emmeline Pankhurst.
(Courtesy of
LSE Library)

being Lady Betty's sister, she did come to Scotland in 1909 and spoke at various meetings to many of the working-class, something she had previously not done. She was imprisoned several times and force-fed.

Mary Crudelius (1839-1877). Although born in Lancashire, her parents were both Scottish. Mary lived in Edinburgh from the age of 11, and when she married, her home was in Leith.

At the age of 27, she was one of 1,500 women who signed the first petition sent to parliament regarding votes for women.

Mary was committed to achieving better higher education for women and, in 1868, was a founder member of the Edinburgh Ladies Education Association (ELEA). The aim was not to give threat to any professional status, but through women attending lectures it was hoped to broaden their minds and give them equal opportunities.

While endeavouring on this venture, she withdrew from active work regarding suffrage, but did write to another suffragette, Agnes

McClaren, stating 'she would still do all that she could, but her real work was dedicated to achievement of education'.

In 1873, women were enrolled on courses such as maths, chemistry and botany.

She was supported by Professor David Masson (who had also helped Sophia Jex-Blake), whose first English Literature course attracted over 250 women, 95 of whom took an examination.

In 1893, eight women graduated from the university and by 1914, more than 1,000 females had graduated.

Sadly, Mary died aged 38 in 1877 and did not see the end result of her tireless work. But surely she must have been happy to see the higher education doors starting to open for her fellow women.

Sarah Elizabeth Siddons Mair (1846-1941) was born in Edinburgh to wealthy parents. Her grandfather and great grandmother were in the acting profession.

In 1865, Sarah founded the Edinburgh Ladies Debating Society, where women discussed social issues concerning their rights and education, expanding their minds, as well as learning how to speak and debate in public. This all took place in the family's dining room.

She eventually became president of the Edinburgh National Society for Women's Suffrage and went on to work with Mary Crudelius in the ELEA. She was instrumental in the late 1800s for offering correspondence courses to women who could not attend university, and she set up St Georges Training College. In 1888 she was governor of the St Georges High School for Girls, which then had fifty pupils. By 1914, the numbers rose to more than 300. Some of the girls from this school were reported to be the first female graduates at Edinburgh University. The Northern Men's Association for Women's Suffrage was conducted in 1910 in the Mairs' home.

The Society for Equal Citizenship was led by Sarah after 1918, when only women over 30 could vote. This was actually the non-militant NUWSS, renamed after the First World War.

Through her efforts in further education for women, Sarah was made a Dame of the British Empire.

Although she died in 1941, her home had still been used for women's welfare and activities.

Priscilla Bright McLaren (1815-1906) was the third wife of radical MP Duncan McLaren, and also prime minister John Bright's sister (John Bright led the anti-corn law campaign). Although born in England, after she married Duncan McLaren in 1848, she spent her married life in Edinburgh.

After MP John Stuart Mill's support for the women's vote and the proposed amendment to the Reform Act of 1867 failed to materialise (only giving male householders more voting powers), Priscilla formed the Edinburgh Society for Women's Suffrage (ESWS).

Priscilla Bright McLaren. (Courtesy of LSE Library)

A great campaigner, in 1870, with her sister-in-law and others, she formed the Ladies National Association, which dealt with the tricky subject of the Contagious Disease Act. Prostitutes were put in lock hospitals if they were proven to have a venereal disease, but the men who visited these women escaped any kind of chastising or were (it appears) not themselves checked to see if they were spreading the infections. Priscilla, along with English feminist Josephine Butler and their fellow women (and some men), fought to have a repeal against the 1867 Act. More than 2,500,000 signatures were presented to the House of Commons for repealing the Act and strongly advocating that double standards were not acceptable. In 1886, the Act was repealed.

In the 1890s, Priscilla, in her role as president of the Scottish Special Appeal Committee, collected an amazing 248,000 signatures in favour of the women's vote to send to parliament.

She died aged 91, but had remained steadfast to the end for women's suffrage.

Dr Agnes McLaren (stepdaughter of Priscilla) (1837-1913) was born in Edinburgh to Duncan McLaren and his second wife Christine Renton. Agnes was only 4 when her mother died, and Priscilla became her stepmother when she was 11 years old.

Suffrage discussions were high on the agenda in the McLaren household, so Agnes grew up with this in mind. In 1867, she became joint secretary of the Edinburgh National Society for Women's Suffrage with Eliza Wigham. She spoke at many meetings throughout Scotland, as far as Orkney and Shetland.

She studied to become a doctor, after meeting Sophia Jex Blake, trained in France and became a member of the Royal College of Dublin. In 1890, she became a member of the WSPU, and was part of the NUWSS election fighting fund three years later.

Agnes was still a member of the Catholic Women's Society for Suffrage when she died aged 76.

Eliza Wigham (1820-1899) was born in Edinburgh to a Quaker family. She became involved, like her mother, in the abolition of slavery. Although a private woman, she was a member of the Edinburgh Ladies Emancipation Society and, in 1867, she became joint secretary, with Agnes McLaren, of the ENSWS (Edinburgh National Society for Womens Suffrage). A caring woman, she often visited the Edinburgh poorhouses, reading to the women, and giving them extra comfort.

A staunch campaigner for women's rights, she was also involved in the repeal of the Contagious Disease Act. She spoke at several meetings in Glasgow and Edinburgh on suffrage.

Other causes she chose to pioneer were the Penny Savings Bank and the Women's Working Society, which were self-help savings schemes to help the poor. She sat with several other females (including McLaren family members) on the ladies committee of Dean Bank Home, which helped destitute girls, thus saving them from a life of crime. Some had been sent there after petty crimes already, and the home was established in order to give the girls/young women an opportunity to recover their position in life.

Although she died aged 79, until her death she was still a member of the executive committee of the NUWSS. Her home is reported to have been another centre for women's activities regarding suffrage. It appears she was a woman who went about her work helping others, never married but felt strongly about women's rights and equality.

Duchess of Atholl (1874-1960) was an anti-suffragist. Born Katharine Marjory Ramsay, in Edinburgh, to an aristocratic family, she was married at 25 to the Marquis of Tullibardine. He became MP for West Perthshire and she, as his dutiful wife (albeit not entirely happy due to his wanderings elsewhere) helped with his political career. She was asked to be president of the West Perthshire Women's Unionist Association.

In 1912 she was involved in the Highlands and Islands Medical Service, which delivered medical service to crofters.

There seems to be some contradiction in Katharine's life as both she and her husband (known as Bardie) were strongly against women's suffrage. They both believed that a woman's place was in the home, and it is reported they both said: 'Women do not want the vote and those with large families had no time for politics.' The duchess was even quoted as saying 'even women tinkers will be allowed to vote'.

Katharine did seek to improve social conditions for women and children in places such as India and Spain. But again, there was a contradiction in her views here in the UK. She supported children working in factories because 'the little hands could get into the machinery'.

However, in 1923 she became MP for the Scottish Unionist Party, the first woman to be elected in Scotland and the first to have a ministerial role in a Tory government.

So why did she not support franchise for women, when she herself went into parliament? Why did she not play the woman's role and stay at home as she and her husband had once said? Historian William Knox felt she had an ignorance and insensitivity to the lives of the British masses. Could it be she had a privileged life and didn't really understand the need for women to have the vote, whatever class they were?

Duncan McLaren (husband to Priscilla McLaren) (1800-1886), **Jacob Bright** (brother to Priscilla) (1821-1899) **and John Stuart Mill** (1806-1873). Duncan was Lord Provost of Edinburgh in 1851 and in 1865 was elected MP for Edinburgh. With his wife Priscilla, he fully supported the women's suffrage cause.

In 1870, along with Priscilla's brother, MP Jacob Bright, and MP John Stuart Mill, he chaired a meeting in Edinburgh to discuss women's suffrage. This meeting was also attended by several male councillors and professionals including Professor Masson. The meeting was recorded as voting unanimously in favour of women suffrage, and John Stuart Mill said: 'The cause owes a debt to Scotland, and Scotland to Edinburgh.'

Duncan and his wife attended the London Women's Suffrage meeting in 1871, and in 1881 he put forward the first Married Women's Property Act (Scotland).

VOTES FOR WOMEN.

JOHN STUART MILL,
PIONEER OF WOMEN'S FREEDOM.

Published by the Women's Freedom League, 1. Robert Street, Adelphi, W.C.

John Stuart Mill.
(Courtesy of LSE
Library)

John Stuart Mill was born in England, but was rector at St Andrews University for three years in the mid-1800s. His wife, Harriet Taylor Mill, was a supporter of women's votes and penned an essay published in 1851 entitled: *Enfranchisement of Women*. Mill was the first MP in parliament to emphasise the need for women to vote.

Bessie Watson (1900-1992) was born in Edinburgh as Elizabeth, but was always known as Bessie. Her photograph has appeared in many suffragette articles and in books, as she was probably one of the youngest females to march in the 1909 procession in Edinburgh. She had taken up bagpipe-playing aged 7.

Suffragette march, Edinburgh. (Courtesy of city of Edinburgh Museums and Galleries)

Edinburgh Banner from Mary Lowndes album. (Courtesy of LSE Library)

Bessie Watson.
(Courtesy of
city of
Edinburgh
Museums
and Gallleries)

Bessie played the bagpipes at the procession and sometimes rode on a float. Christabel Pankhurst presented her with a Queen Boudica brooch that same year.

In 1911, she played with other pipers at the 5-mile-long Great Pageant in London. A keen supporter of women's rights, she even played outside the jails where suffragettes were imprisoned. The brooch she received from Christabel she gave to Margaret Thatcher when she became the first female prime minister in 1979.

CHAPTER TWO

Glasgow

Brief history from the eighteenth century

The name Glasgow is believed to be Gaelic meaning 'Welsh Glas' or Beloved Green Place, although the earliest known name for Glasgow was Cathures.

St Mungo, also known as Kentigern, founded Glasgow in the sixth century and is its patron saint. Even then women did not have it easy. Kentigern was the product of his mother's rape by a cousin and, unfortunately, she was sent into exile. St Mungo went on to be a bishop.

Glasgow is set on the banks of the River Clyde. It was originally a small town, but when the River Clyde had rock removed from its watery beds in the mid-1800s, it enabled big ships to enter the dock. Previously, due to the shallow waters, only smaller vessels could enter. This in turn led to more trade in and out of Glasgow. It was once the second city of Scotland for production, dealing with locomotives, ships and cars.

Population of the city and surrounding areas as follows:-

1831 = 202,426	small area of 8.83km²
1872 = 494,824	area increase to 24.42km²
1901 = 761,712	area increase to 51.35km²
1921 = 1,034,174	area increase to 77.63km²
1971 = 897,485	area increase to 160.77km²
2001 = 586,710	area increase to 177.30km²
2011 = 599,650	area decrease to 174.70km²
2016 = 615,070	

The ratio of women to men throughout the timeline appears to be approximately fifty-one per cent women to forty-nine per cent men.

In the 1830s and 1840s, large numbers of Irish male and female migrants came to Glasgow to escape the potato famine.

Daniel Defoe described Glasgow in the late 1700s as 'the cleanest and most beautiful city in Britain, excepting London'. This, however, was to change.

Working life

Due to the War of Independence in America (1775-1783), these colonies were lost to Britain, and tobacco, which had been a thriving trade in Glasgow, ceased and some companies went bankrupt. Linen (as with other big Scottish towns and cities) came to the forefront, but became unobtainable around 1780.

In the late 1790s and beyond, there were more than forty large mills surrounding Glasgow. These were mainly cotton, but later jute and wool were also developed. There was one water-powered mill at Woodside, Glasgow. Prior to this, half of the 4,000-plus people employed in the textile industry were women and children. From 1812, more than 151,000 people were employed to work from home and, in 1840, the majority were then working in the mills. For employers it was a form of cheap labour.

Just outside Glasgow were the Calton Weavers, who had been established since late 1700s. Women, children and men worked extremely long hours to survive, often selling their bedding and personal belongings to earn a crust. Due to the power-loom factories the hand-loomers faced a life of destitution. Riots ensued at the power-loom factories when hand-weavers attacked them with stones in the early 1800s.

The desperate situation that occurred in 1810 was the owner's refusal to employ further female apprentices (unless from a weaver's family), due to the fact the male workers felt threatened by women workers.

Twenty-three years later the situation worsened when female spinners were violently forced out by the Calton men. Wages over the years had decreased for the long hours (normally thirteen per day) from 18 shillings to 8 shillings for a six-day week. The men viewed the women as competition.

Templeton Carpet Factory, built in the late 1880s in Calton, employed women workers but, unfortunately, twenty-nine females were killed when a wall in the construction process collapsed. Disaster struck females again in 1900 when a fire killed several in the factory. A female stone figure stands perched on top of the building representing the women who were killed.

Middle-class women in the 1800s did take on several roles, but were classed as wives of business males such as stationers and accountants. It seems their roles were secondary to their husbands'. Stanley and Carnarvon Streets in Glasgow were home to lodgers of middle-class households. This was the women helping to bring income to the house. It appears many of the them had no occupation, but in 1891 sixteen households run by the women took in boarders in those streets. Research into post office directories and valuation rolls by Eleanor Gordon (in 1985) found that some middle-class women worked as plumbers, dentists, photographers, accountants and coal dealers, to name just a few occupations. However, most of these businesses were run on a small scale. One large business was a tearooms owned by Miss Kate Cranston, a name still spoken of highly today in Glasgow. Miss Cranston's tea and luncheon rooms provided women a place to eat and chat away from the men. That said, she also had a room for the gentlemen for smoking or playing billiards. In Glasgow, women made up six per cent of shop owners in the later eighteenth century. They included grocery stores, milliners, dairies and working on market stalls. Women often sold wares from the front rooms of their houses. In particular, Maryhill seems to have seen this practice often. The 1851 census shows that teachers and governesses were the top employment for women and, in 1891, dressmakers were more prevalent amongst females, followed by teachers, shop assistants and clerical workers.

In 1883, at Paisley Mill, the owners sacked some women in preference of men. They reckoned on the women being docile and not protesting. However, three women were jailed for picketing. It was events such as this that made many women fight for equality and better working conditions, which in turn gave females the impetus to take action in women's rights for the vote.

Women also helped to run family businesses, such as bakers, hatters, brewers and suchlike, and when husbands died, some widows took over completely. As a married woman in the eighteenth and nineteenth centuries, any property, investments, etc., a female owned before she was married were usually taken over by her husband. The wife lived under the husband's protection, and he appeared to own everything. Her condition was known as coverture. However, over the period 1870-1893, several updates on the Married Women's Act came into force, which gave females more rights to property and investments.

Women on the home front. (Courtesy of LSE Library)

It appears there was discrimination for female workers in Glasgow between the two world wars, as most male applicants were offered jobs, but only a small proportion of women were taken on.

Interestingly, Glasgow Subway opened in 1896, but women were unable to work as drivers. This only changed in 1980. They were, however, allowed to work as booking office assistants, according to Glasgow Transport Museum.

Only six per cent of married women in Glasgow were working in 1921 compared to Dundee's twenty-four per cent.

So, despite women's efforts in maintaining several workforces while the men were away fighting in both wars, it seems many of the positions they secured during those times often did not remain afterwards.

Health & welfare

As already seen, poverty, pollution, poor housing and lack of sanitation were abundant in nineteenth-century Scotland as a whole. This, in turn, led to many diseases such as cholera, typhus and smallpox. A cholera epidemic occurred in 1832 and approximately 5,000 people died from it. Deaths were also recorded in the surrounding areas of Glasgow. Another epidemic caused more deaths in 1847/8.

In Glasgow there could be as many as twelve to sixteen people living in a room, due to lack of housing. With poor ventilation and sanitation, and often damp and cramped facilities, respiratory disease and tuberculosis accounted for two-fifths of Glasgow deaths in the 1860s.

In 1855, a parliamentary Act allowed water to be drawn from Loch Katrine to improve the public water supply. Cholera struck in 1865/6, but this time, due to the improved water supply, fewer deaths were recorded.

In 1898, infant mortality was dire. In the Gorbals area, for every 1,000 births, 200 babies died.

In the 1800s, prostitution, which sometimes led to venereal disease, was on the increase. Many of the women were forced into this work due to poverty or because of drink issues, and some may have believed they would attract a rich man and become a kept woman. Some nineteenth-century doctors prescribed fornication to middle-class males who suffered from tension.

Drink was a major problem with men and often led to battered wives. The medical officer for Glasgow Prison in 1812, Mr James Devon, was quoted as saying that 'drink, crime and overcrowding in a rented slum go together'.

Often women led a life of drudgery. Isolated at home with the children and domestic chores, the husband worked and drank to escape the miseries of life. Then, while drunk, the husband beat his wife. Perhaps an all-too-common tale back then, and still even today.

Unfortunately cleanliness was not common with people in general, thus causing the further spread of diseases.

Barnhill Poorhouse in Glasgow was one of the largest in Scotland. In the 1881 census, a total of 1,193 mixed gender and age inmates were recorded, with twenty-four staff employed, nineteen of whom were female. In 1920, there were 2,000 inmates with sixty staff, these being equal male and female.

It appears men were given priority regarding the National Insurance Acts 1911/12. As they were regarded as the breadwinner of the family they were treated, but wives and children were not entitled to the same.

Things had to change, and 1919 saw schemes for maternity and child welfare come to fruition. Only just over half the populated areas were originally covered, but increased in 1929. However, even in 1939, there was still an issue over beds in hospitals for children and pregnant women.

Education

Girls from working-class families were often never afforded the luxury of schooling. Most working-class men in the nineteenth century were allowed to learn basic literary skills. Some boys also. If girls were given instruction at school, it was more often on domestic training, as their future was seen as marriage and child-rearing and little else. Teaching the girls classics was considered a waste of time.

The Church of Scotland and local landowners paid for some schools, but it is believed in the mid-1800s that 20,000 children in Glasgow were not in the reach of educational organisations. Due to the poverty, parents often sent their children to earn rather than learn. It was estimated that fewer than fifty per cent of children aged 5 to 10 received education in the mid-1800s.

The Education Act of 1872 changed the perspective. It was then compulsory for ages 5-13 to attend school. However, secondary education was not provided for the working classes. Twenty years later, secondary education became free, but sadly only a small percentage took up the opportunity. Most 14-year-olds went to work.

Females in the mid-1800s accounted for only thirty-five per cent of the teaching profession. But in the early 1900s, this changed to predominantly females at seventy per cent. They were, of course, cheaper to employ with salaries half that of male teachers' pay.

Education for women was often helped by other women who realised the inequality of it all.

Isabella Elder (1828-1905) was born in the Gorbals, Glasgow. In 1857, she married John Elder, who ran a widely acclaimed ship-building yard. After twelve years of marriage, she was left a childless but wealthy widow.

In 1883, Isabella bought North Park House, Glasgow, and gifted the building to Queen Margaret's College for the use of higher education for women. It was eleven years later that the first Scottish graduate for medicine was achieved at the college, and Isabella, who had helped to finance this, was able to see her kindness come to fruition.

When Isabella died in 1905, **Dr Marion Gilchrist** signed the death certificate. A fitting tribute to Isabella, as Marion was the first graduate of medicine in Glasgow. The same college that Isabella had helped finance.

Isabella Elder.
(Courtesy of
Glasgow University
Archives)

Some schools selectively picked pupils for education, such as St Mungo's Academy and Hillhead High School as reported in M. Meighan's book on Glasgow. But after 1972, selection for children was abolished. Certainly, females benefited from the O-level grading from 1962 onwards, and more girls went on to higher education.

Suffrage, politics, women and notable men

It is fair to say that some working-class women before 1918 were faced with the drudgery of life and failed to see how the vote would change anything. As with all areas in Scotland, Glasgow had many suffragettes, and feminism was just as strong in this part of the UK.

Replica badge.
(Courtesy of city
of Edinburgh
Museums and
Galleries)

Marion Kirkland Reid (1815-1902) was born in Glasgow. Marion
was one of the earlier feminists in history who believed in rights
for women. The term suffrage had not yet been conceived, but for
a woman of her time this was surely the commencement of the
road to enfranchisement. She wrote a book in 1843 entitled *Plea
for a Woman*, in which she advocated women voting in a bid to
change laws and legal discrimination. She describes how women's
education and jobs were 'evil and unjust'. She goes on to say:

> Man and woman are the same, they are alike moral, accountable and
> immortal beings; and it is on this account that they are entitled to the
> same rights.

There is very little personal information on Marion, apart from
her marriage to Hugo Reid in Edinburgh in 1839. They had one
daughter. Marion died in Hammersmith, London, aged 87.

She was a steadfast 'rock' in the road to votes for women and equality.

Helen Crawfurd (1877-1954) was born in the Gorbals, Glasgow. She married twice. Helen's interest in suffrage commenced in 1900 when she was appalled by the lack of women's education. As a member of the non-militant NUWSS, regular meetings were held in her Glasgow house. She believed if mothers of the race had a say, then things might change. However, 1910 saw Helen switch her allegiance to the more militant WSPU in Rutherglen, south of Glasgow. She felt the militant tactics would achieve results.

Fiona Jack with her great aunt Helen Crawfurd.

Between 1910 and 1914 she was imprisoned four times in response to her inflammatory remarks (one being at the Liberal leader for education) and window smashing. On each occasion she went on hunger strike. She opposed the First World War and became a member of the Independent Labour Party (ILP).

The famous 1915 rent strike in Glasgow saw Helen and female colleagues set up the Women's Peace Crusade (WPC), and they joined the 10,000-strong march through Glasgow protesting against private landlords increasing rents. The shocked government brought in the Rent Restrictions Act, which in turn froze rents for the working classes.

Later, she became involved with the Communist Party of Great Britain, and in retirement at the age of 69 she became the first woman councillor in Dunoon. She kept this position for two years before taking ill. Helen died aged 77, but had led an energetic political life to the end.

Her great niece, Fiona Jack, an artist living in New Zealand, keeps her memory alive and last year held various talks about Helen at Glasgow Women's Library.

Anna Rhoda Craig (sometimes also known as Robinson or Greig) was born in Gravesend, but when she married a dock worker in 1899, she moved to Glasgow. She became secretary for Dumbarton WSPU.

In 1912, Rhoda was arrested in connection with breaking a car window in which she thought Winston Churchill had been travelling whilst visiting Glasgow. She was sentenced at Glasgow Sheriff Court to ten days' imprisonment.

Two years later, she was involved in arson at St Fillians, with the burning of a mansion called Allt-an-Fhionn. The property owned by Mr and Mrs Stirling Boyd was completely destroyed. Mrs Boyd supported anti-suffrage, so was that the probable reason for such a drastic action? Two other large properties were also damaged by fire around the same period. It was thought Rhoda was one of the arsonists. Although again imprisoned, she went on hunger strike but was eventually released due to lack of evidence, only to be charged again for starting a fire in a wood plantation in Dumbartonshire.

A spokeswoman for suffrage at the time remarked on the militant actions of its members: 'Strong, sporting instincts among women, they will take, as well as give any blows that are going.'

It seems Rhoda was one of those women.

Dr Elizabeth Dorothea Chalmers-Smith (1872-1944) graduated in medicine from Glasgow University at the age of 22, going on to work at the Samaritan Hospital for Women. At the age of 29, she married a minister and went on to have six children.

She, along with Ethel Moorhead, attempted to start a Glasgow house fire in July 1913. But both women were arrested. In two separate incidents she went on hunger strike, was released under the 'Cat & Mouse Act', but failed both times to return. She was never caught again. Her minister husband did not support her actions and consequently divorced her, keeping their two sons with him. Dorothea left taking their four daughters with her.

On 29 July 1913, Dorothea received a silver medal from the WSPU 'for gallant action whereby through endurance to last extremity of hunger and hardship, a great principle of political justice was vindicated'. The medal now resides at the Glasgow Museum.

Dr Marion Gilchrist (1864-1952) was born in Bothwell, east of Glasgow. She never married but at the age of 30 was one of the first female medical graduates in Scotland.

The unique Queen Margaret College, Glasgow, commenced in 1883 and trained women in arts and medicine. The university, despite the University Act of 1889, had declined to train females, so the college ran the courses as separate facilities to the men.

Clinical work for female students was on two wards at the Royal Infirmary, but they still encountered problems while training. The Western Infirmary refused them entry, the Victoria Infirmary (closed in 2018) had shelved then the idea of female medical students, and the maternity hospital taught some clinical training for females on limited approval.

Marion Gilchrist
1894, author
unknown.
(University
of Glasgow
Library)

Opposition to female clinicians was due to no appropriate toilet facilities, no recreational facilities (despite several female nurses), mental capacity lacking and a poor education, and it was thought that females were of a 'delicate' nature and would make poor doctors. Despite all this, Marion qualified in 1894 and went on to specialise in ophthalmics.

In 1902, she was one of the founding members of the Glasgow and West Scotland Association for Women's Suffrage (along with Grace Patterson) but they, along with other members, were becoming disillusioned with the lack of achievement (they thought) of the group. Marion left and joined the WSPU in 1907. She was also the first chairwoman of the Glasgow branch of the British Medical Division.

Jessie Stephens (1893-1979) was from a working-class background. Some reports say she was born in London and then lived in Edinburgh, but her roots also seem to have been in Glasgow. She wanted to be a teacher, but family circumstances meant she had to earn a living working as a domestic servant in Glasgow.

As a member of the Independent Labour Party (ILP), she organised the maidservants into a union in 1912, which was followed by the formation of the Scottish Domestic Workers Union in 1913.

At the age of 20, she was an active member of the WSPU and frequently posted acid into letterboxes. She appeared to go undetected as she wore her maid's outfit and blended in with the crowds.

Jessie spoke to historian Brian Harrison in the 1970s and told him that the acid was given by a female chemist who did not want to do the deed but was happy to help in this way.

She was one of the youngest members of the WSPU to lobby the House of Commons and was actively involved in various organisations, such as the National Federation of Women Workers, campaigning for women rights in the workplace.

Agnes Lennox was a Chartist in the early 1800s in Glasgow. Chartism was a working class movement between 1838-48 that was aimed at gaining political rights. As chairwoman of the Gorbals Female Universal Suffrage Society that supported their menfolk in the cause for male suffrage, Agnes also believed women had rights to politics participation. Many of the men felt women should vote, but this was not part of the Chartist beliefs.

In the draft People's Charter manifesto, a clause recommended that women should have enfranchisement. However, some members of the London Working Men's Association (whose draft it was) had this removed as they thought it may hinder the suffrage of the men.

The Gorbals Society had more than forty members, many of whom were from the working class.

Jane Smeal, although not a suffragette deserves a mention as she was a Chartist like Agnes (above). Born in Glasgow, she was involved in the early 1800s with anti-slavery. She went on to help

with universal suffrage. In 1838, along with her English friend
Elizabeth Pease, she wrote a pamphlet entitled *Address to the
women of Great Britain*. They wanted women to form political
associations in the bid to abolish slavery. Were these the first steps
to women's votes? These were ordinary women fighting for causes
they believed in.

Her father William Smeal was a Quaker and president of the
Emancipation Society in Glasgow. His vice chairman publicly
resigned in anger over comments about women's suffrage. Smeal,
in order to win him back, said they neither approved or disapproved.
This in turn angered the Ladies Auxiliary Emancipation Society,
with which his daughter was involved.

Frances Gordon was a suffragette arrested for arson on a house
in Lanarkshire in 1914. The caretaker was woken at 2.30am and
locked Frances into the kitchen until the police arrived and she was
arrested. The female owner apparently did not want to prosecute,
but it seems the case had already been put forward for trial.

She was one of the imprisoned suffragettes who suffered badly
at the hands of a Doctor Hugh Ferguson-Watson in Perth prison.
Like other suffragettes, she went on hunger strike and was then
forcibly fed. A metal clamp kept her mouth open and a long tube
was inserted into her stomach, and thus fluid food entered. It has
been reported that she was also fed rectally.

Maggie Moffatt (1883-1942) was born in England, but her family
moved back to Glasgow when she was young. She was the wife of
Glasgow actor, director and writer Graham Moffatt, they married
in 1897. She was a member of the WSPU and in 1907 marched into
London to demonstrate at the House of Commons and was arrested.
When asked for his views on the situation, her husband Graham
said he was very proud of her. She spent two weeks in Holloway
and was one of the first women from Scotland to be imprisoned.

Maggie eventually joined the WFL as she did not like the
WSPU's militant actions. Due to their professional workload, the
WFL were latterly only active regarding suffrage in comments to
the press.

Graham Moffatt (1866-1951) was born in Glasgow. He founded the Men's League for Women's Suffrage in Glasgow in 1907.

In October 1909, he marched in a demonstration in Edinburgh, in support of women's suffrage. On 6 November that year he presented his play *The Maid and the Magistrate* to the WFL members-only event. It was a play all about suffrage.

He retired to South Africa with his wife Maggie and daughter Winifred.

Keir Hardie (1856-1915) was born in Newtown, North Lanarkshire, east of Glasgow.

He came from a working-class background and began working as a messenger boy for a shipping company in Govan, aged 7.

He was first inspired by the Liberal party, but some years later, at the age of 37, he became the first leader of the ILP in London. He was disillusioned by Liberal policies, believing they did not support the working classes.

He was also a great supporter of women's suffrage. In the late 1800s, he was arrested at one of their meetings, but the Home Secretary had him released.

Many of his fellow MPs did not agree with his support of women's suffrage. In 1907, Hardie complained in the House of Commons on the brutality of the force-feeding of suffragette prisoners. He said:

> Women weak and worn down by hunger, are seized upon, held down by brute force, gagged, a tube inserted down their throats, and food poured or pumped into their stomachs.

This was documented in 1909 in a letter Hardie wrote to *Votes for Women* newspaper.

Despite Hardie being married with four children to Lillias Wilson, it appears he also had some sort of relationship with Sylvia Pankhurst, who was almost half his age. However, he seems to have been a man of integrity regarding women's suffrage, and tried to support the women's cause.

CHAPTER THREE

Dundee and Perth

Brief history

Dundee is on the banks of the north River Tay and is the fourth largest city in Scotland. It has been around since the late Iron Age. There are conflicting views on where the name Dundee came from. Some believe it came from the word dun which meant 'fort', and the latter part of the word derived from 'tay' (Duntay). There are several other possibilities too. Edinburgh is 60 miles to the south and Aberdeen 67 miles to the north.

Dundee has always been famous for three things: jam (or marmalade), jute and journalism.

Janet Keiller established the marmalade in 1797, but it is believed this was adapted from an earlier recipe for marmalade in the sixteenth century (Monty Don, the gardening celebrity, is Janet's great-great-great-great-grandson). The marmalade was shipped worldwide under the company name of James Keiller & Sons. When none of the menfolk were left to run the business, Janet carried on with the help of her daughter-in-law Margaret, proving that back in the 1800s women were capable of 'holding their own'. The company also manufactured the famous Dundee cake.

Dundee is well-known for its jute industry, although textiles (such as linen) in general were also common in the area. The whaling industry from the city's port was helpful with the manufacture of jute. Whale oil was a necessity in order to work the jute on machinery. In 1970, the last jute mill closed.

DC Thomson Publishing, founded by David Coupar Thomson in 1905, is still a family concern to this date. In 1894, the company funded two female journalists to travel the world and write-up reports, which were published in the *Weekly News* and the *Courier*.

Women's World columns were also written in the newspapers at the time, by women, and these often reported on suffrage.

At present the company employs more than 2,000 workers and produces more than 200 publications, including the *Dundee Courier*.

Dundee is also famous for RRS *Discovery*, the ship built in the city between 1871 and 1881. The ship was used by naval officer Robert Falcon Scott to run an expedition to Antarctica.

The Tay Bridge connecting Dundee with Wormit, Fife, across the Firth of Tay, was built in 1878 and at the time was the longest bridge in the world. However, this original bridge collapsed in high winds just after Christmas 1879, killing seventy-five people. They never survived the icy waters of the Firth of Tay. The current bridge was built in 1887, with a refurbishment in 2003.

The approximate population for Dundee was as follows:

1851	Males = 29,755	Females = 35,349
1911	Males = 74,165	Females = 93,145
1971	Males = 94,777	Females = 73,077
1981	Males = 83,718	Females = 65,189
2011	Males = 70,706	Females = 76,562
2016	Males = 71,432	Females = 76,838

Dundee City Council believes the reason for the drop in population figures in 1981 could be due to electoral boundary changes. It may also be due to higher emigration in the 1980s. As with most areas, the proportion of females to men is always slightly higher.

Perth was often called the 'Fair City' after Sir Walter Scott penned *The Fair Maid of Perth*. 'Perth' is a Pictish word meaning thorny woodland. The River Tay runs through Perth city.

The population in 1750 was just 15,000. In 1851 it was 23,835, in 2008 the figure was 44,820 and in 2011 it was 46,970 (city north & south). Again, female numbers were slightly higher than male.

In 1812, Perth prison was built and this, over the years, housed many suffragettes and caused a great deal of anger with the way the women were treated: forcibly fed by a nasal tube as well as rectally. One placard placed in a window before a royal visit simply said 'Visit your Majesty's torture chamber in Perth prison'.

In July 1914, a 24-hour picket was staged outside the prison in support of suffragettes. More than 3,000 women attended.

Working life

In the mid-1850s, larger ships were coming into the new docks, which in turn meant more imported flax and larger quantities of linen exported. This led to numerous women workers in Dundee. Approximately 8,000 women out of a workforce of more than 11,000 were employed within 8 power-loom factories, 62 hand-loom factories and 43 spinning mills.

Women were cheap to employ and were paid terrible wages for long hours. They were lucky if they were paid 5 shillings per week (25 pence). Hand-spinners were usually paid 1 shilling and tuppence.

According to Verdant Works Museum, Dundee, which was originally The High Mill of Verdant Works owned by David Lindsay, because many women worked in the various mills, a great number of men stayed at home tending the children. They were known as 'kettle bilers'.

Life for the women and children working in the mills was hard. Accidents happened. One was in 1852, at Verdant, when a female was caught in a carding machine and unfortunately died. There were other medical issues from working in the factories, which will be covered under the health section.

Dundee was named 'She town' and 'Juteopolis'. The former name was due to the fact the women working in the mills had to adapt to being tough, and the latter was due to jute being the largest employer in the city until the 1950s. Most employees working at the mills didn't get Christmas Day off until 1956.

In other cities, when women married, their employment was limited to jobs such as teaching, and men were assumed to have the ability to 'keep' their wives. However, in Dundee there was a great demand for females, married or single. In employment statistics, married women featured more prominently than in other Scottish towns and cities.

Male workers appeared to have had the skilled jobs at the mills, such as beamers, dressers and authoritarian positions, which meant they earned more money. It couldn't possibly be that women, who worked hard at their jobs, could do the same work as the men. If that was so then the jute barons who owned the mills would have to pay the same wage as they did to the men. This was (at this stage) not going to happen.

As well as working at the mills, women were often used as seasonal labourers for the whaling industry. According to Matt Ylitalo, St Andrews University, Dundee, every social class was involved with whaling. Some females were shareholders, investors or creditors and they often dealt with independent business transactions with the whaling companies.

As with all cities, women were employed in domestic service in Dundee. In fact, two young maidservants addressed a meeting in 1872 at Mathers Hotel, Dundee, calling for better working conditions in domestic service. Thus, the Dundee and District Domestic Servants' Association was formed.

Many men felt that the women should not be demanding change. However, women felt the long hours, little leisure time and their almost total control by the mistresses of the house warranted change. If the jute mill women could stand up for their rights, then so could domestic service females.

According to the census in 1911, female workers in Dundee accounted for fifty per cent of the labour workforce. Out of that percentage, sixty-five per cent were employed in the mills. Domestic service and retail were each represented by six per cent of the females. Employment, such as nursing, teaching, food processing and clothing, accounted for only three per cent of the Dundee female population in the late nineteenth century.

So again, looking at employment in this area, although no direct involvement with suffrage, it is fair to say that these women, along with other Scottish women were (for the main part) not going to be downtrodden. Feminism was definitely raising its head. This in turn would eventually lead to women having the vote.

In Perth, the linen industry faired very well. Dyeing and bleaching were two other areas. Pullars Factory in Perth was a dyer and cleaner of fabrics and was established in 1824. The company employed several women workers and, in 1907, a demand for better wages was staged by the girls from the ironing department. However, this was never addressed.

Some of the women joined the National Federation of Women Workers (NFWW) and over the years Pullars saw many strikes for better wages and working conditions, until 1943 when the company was taken over.

Bells and Dewars whisky distillers were also founded in Perth.

Health & welfare

As with all major cities and towns in Scotland, cholera, typhus, whooping cough, measles and diphtheria were all virulent in the nineteenth century. In 1832, cholera struck and it was said that grave-diggers could not dig the graves quickly enough for the numbers of people dying. So a mass grave was dug in the Howff (graveyard in Dundee). Sadly, people were buried, albeit in their own coffins, but in rows and rows.

In Dundee, whooping cough claimed more than fifty children under the age of 5 in 1896. Diarrhoea in the same year claimed twenty-three children of the same age bracket. Poor sanitation and dirty water led to this symptom which, in turn, led to dehydration. Children, as with the elderly, were (and still are) the most vulnerable of the age groups.

Dundee surprisingly only had five public toilets for its 91,000-plus residents in 1861. Three of these were in hotels. Not everyone had access to windows, so were lacking in natural light and vitamin D from the sun, and poor ventilation.

Ladywell was the main source of water but, unfortunately, this became contaminated with debris from the slaughterhouse, consequently leading to further disease and infection.

In Dundee, seventy-two per cent of the population in the early 1900s lived in cramped one- or two-room houses with several people sharing the accommodation, again leading to poor health. It is reported that some schoolchildren in 1900s Dundee had impaired hearing and poor eyesight due to overcrowding.

For the women who worked in the mills, respiratory conditions were rife due to the dust and 'stour'.

It clogged their noses, mouths, eyes and ears. Some mill workers went deaf due to the loud noise of the machinery. A condition known as 'mill fever', or 'brown lung disease', was caused by inhaling cotton, flax, hemp or jute. Then, of course, where there was machinery (and not the health and safety there is today), accidents did occur.

With the wet spinning, the women and children had sore, chapped hands due to the constant wet and hot spray.

Wages were not good for the women's long hours, hence money could not be spent on luxuries such as meat. Potatoes and porridge were a mainstay of the diet. But there does appear to have been a camaraderie among the mill workers.

It has also been noted that widowhood was a chief cause of poverty.

Poorhouses, such as the Dundee East, were built in 1856 and housed over 800 paupers, 100 lunatics and 100 sick people. This one was governed by Mr Gunn (no experience, he was originally a wine merchant), and the matron was his wife. She was paid a mere £25 per year, compared to his own £79 per year (there is no record of whether she had previous experience). In 1864, the Western Poorhouse (Liff & Benvie) in Dundee housed the more elderly, insane and infirm residents. It was a hard life for all concerned.

The Dundee and District Rescue Home was established for women under 20 in 1877. Prostitution as in many Victorian cities was a way of life for some fallen women, although the problem in Dundee was not as great as in other Scottish cities.

Single mill females often stayed in cheap lodgings and research documents show that managers of these establishments worried that the girls were often vulnerable and seduced.

Education

In 1834, it was calculated that only one-fifteenth of Dundee children attended school. Child labour in those times appears to be why they were not educated. They were cheap to employ and, for instance in the mills, their little hands could get into areas that the adults' hands couldn't.

Before 1914 and the First World War, girls aged 12 to 14 were employed in Dundee, 5,000 working part-time (half-timers), and some girls, if they had passed necessary standards at school were exempt from attending education in the day, in preference to working.

For girls aged 13 and upwards, working full-time in the mill consisted of starting at 6am and finishing at 6pm for five days a week. They were allowed a total of two hours for meals, but then had to attend schooling from 7.15-9.15pm, until aged 14. A long gruelling day for anyone, let along girls of that age. Unfortunately, it was the parents who were poor who often required their children to work in order to 'make ends meet' for the family.

Mary Anne Baxter (1801-1884), a wealthy woman whose family were involved with textiles, was co-founder of the university college of Dundee, which opened four years after her death in 1888. She had stated that the education was for both sexes to study science, literature and fine arts. Two well-known females educated at the college were Mary Lily Walker, who helped women and children in their working conditions in industry, and Margaret Fairlie (1891-1963), Scotland's first female professor, who worked in gynaecology.

Churches in Scotland played a role in the education of children before the 1872 Education Act, but it appears mainly education of boys was thought relevant. Dame schools (ladies ran as a business teaching the 3Rs) did cater for some girls and boys, but usually after age 7 they went on to burgh schools.

The Education Act saw the introduction of school boards running the schools, but they were fee-paying. It wasn't until 1890 that fees were abolished.

Unfortunately, according to Friends of Dundee Archives, girls were often taught silence, modesty and obedience, and were often quite illiterate. It was thought education 'might damage their brains', and their learning consisted mainly of preparation for marriage and home-making.

In Perth Academy in 1866, figures show that there were no working-class children in education there. As with most towns and cities of the time, the lower class children were sent off to work, for many their wages helped their families 'get by'.

Suffrage, politics, women and notable men

Dundee was the first Scottish city to imprison suffragettes, who often went on hunger strike and were then force-fed.

Several acts of militancy occurred in Dundee, such as Farrington Hall being burnt down in May 1913 by the suffragettes. They claimed responsibility by sending the police a copy of *Suffragette* with the message 'Farrington Hall – a protest again British Tyranny, blames Asquith & Co'. All were reported in the *Scotsman* and *Dundee Advertiser* newspapers. All that remains of the 1854 Gothic mansion originally built for a jute baron are a few masonry pieces and two gate pierheads.

In 1914, Dudhope Castle in Dundee would have been burnt down by suffragettes had it not been for the fuse to the bomb fizzling out.

King George V and Queen Mary, who visited the city in July 1914, were also on the receiving end of the suffragettes. (See below under Olive Walton.)

Ethel Moorhead (1870-1955) spent her early years in Kent, but after travelling for her father's work as an army surgeon she, with her parents, lived in Dundee from 1900. As well as a suffragette she was a talented artist, undertaking training in Paris. Although now demolished, she had an art studio in Kings Street Arcade, Dundee.

Ethel joined the WSPU in 1910, but her first claim to fame was in December that year when she threw an egg at the Home Secretary,

Winston Churchill, in protest of his ordering of the force-feeding of suffragettes.

Ethel went on to take various actions that unfortunately had her put in prison several times. At one political meeting the women were jostled by men, and she was apparently hit in the ribs by a male teacher from Broughton School. A little while later she went to accost him at his school with a whip, but he managed to stop her and a charge was brought against her. She paid the £1 fine.

During 1912 she smashed the Wallace glass case at the memorial tower, broke glass windows at a Thomas Cook outlet, then threw a stone at a car she believed Lloyd George was in. This cost her several detainments in Stirling jail and Perth prison.

Not deterred, in 1913 she threw pepper in the face of a policeman in Cupar, Fife. Following her arrest and detainment, she then broke cell windows, flooded prison passageways and went on hunger strike.

After release, later that same year, in Glasgow she was caught with fire-lighting equipment and was further sentenced to eight months' imprisonment, but released under the 'Cat & Mouse Act' after going on hunger strike again. However, it was in 1914 that Ethel got into real trouble. She was apprehended after appearing outside the fifteenth-century stately home Traquair House, south of Edinburgh. She was quizzed by the housekeeper, who was suspicious of her and her friend (due to fires started at mansions by suffragettes).

She was arrested and placed in Calton Jail, Edinburgh, and eventually force-fed, after going on hunger strike in February. This was the first time a suffragette had been forcibly fed in Scotland. Dr Ferguson Watson was the medic who performed the procedure, but Ethel was released after the eighth time of force-feeding due to contracting double pneumonia. Doctor Grace Cadell, who then became her custodian, was appalled, as she believed Ethel's illness was due to the feeding tube being inserted incorrectly into Ethel's lungs rather than stomach. This was always vehemently denied by the prison authorities. They said the prisoner smashed cell windows and tore her clothes off, thus causing the pneumonia.

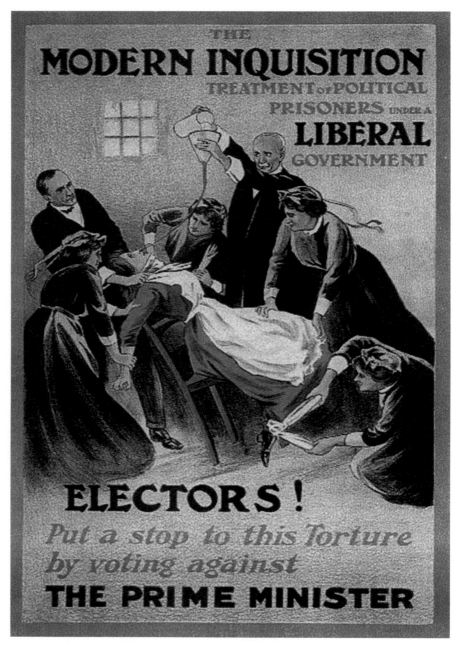

Force feeding poster. (Courtesy of city of Edinburgh Museums and Galleries)

Huge uproars were caused because of this event. Reports in newspapers such as the *Edinburgh Evening Dispatch* printed the headline 'Scotland disgraced and dishonoured'.

It was believed that the burning of the medieval White Kirk in East Lothian was a direct result of Ethel's force-feeding. **Janie Allan** (Glasgow suffragette) even wrote so to the chairman of the Prison Commission. Ethel recovered and went on to run the Women's Freedom League National Service Organisation after the war.

Isabella Carrie (1878-1981). Some say school teacher Isabella was a quiet, unassuming woman, who only went to a women's Liberal meeting to hear what Winston Churchill had to say. It was well known he was not in favour of women's votes. He once said in 1874 to Prime Minister Asquith 'that women were well represented by husbands, brothers and fathers'.

Isabella was apparently incensed when Churchill made some flippant remark about women at the meeting she attended. She got up and shouted something at him and was manhandled by male stewards and thrown onto the steps outside. She always maintained if she wasn't a suffragette when she went in, she was now.

Although not militant in her actions, Isabella gave refuge to several suffragettes, and she was supposed to house Emmeline Pankhurst on a visit to Dundee. But Mrs Pankhurst was actually arrested in Glasgow before she reached Dundee.

Isabella went onto to live past the ripe old age of 100, dying in Broughty Ferry.

Olive Walton (1876-1937) lived in Tunbridge Wells, England, but became a Dundee WSPU organiser in 1913. When King George and Queen Mary visited Dundee in July 1914, she threw a ball with an attached petition into the royal carriage while they were visiting a flax works in Dundee. She hoped the king would stop the force-feeding of suffragettes. She was arrested but the queen did not want to take proceedings further. On her release, Olive managed a second attempt when the queen was in Edinburgh.

She joined the Women Police Volunteers in 1914 and became only one of four inspectors at the headquarters of the Women's Police Service. After working in Dublin, she retired due to a motorbike accident while on duty.

Olive never married, but adopted a daughter, Christabel.

Fanny Parker (1875-1924) was born in New Zealand but came to the UK in 1896 to study as a teacher in Cambridge. Her uncle was Lord Kitchener. New Zealand gave votes to women in 1893, so that may have spurred Fanny on to join WSPU in 1908. She was arrested and spent time in Holloway Prison that year, but her connection with Scotland was in 1909 when she was a speaker for Scottish Universities Women's Suffrage Union.

She was to become an organiser for WSPU in Dundee in late 1912, after being organiser for Glasgow in 1912. The lady certainly moved around as she was arrested in December of that year in Aberdeen. Fanny, along with other suffragettes, had tried to cause an affray at a music hall where Lloyd George was holding a meeting. She was arrested and imprisoned, but after a hunger strike lasting five days, she was released. However, Fanny's militancy was far from over. In 1914 she tried to set fire to Robbie Burns' cottage, in Alloway, Ayr, with another suffragette believed to be Ethel Moorhead. A night watchman at the premises foiled the attempt at 2.30am and Fanny was caught, while her accomplice escaped.

She was originally imprisoned in Ayr but then transferred 100 miles away to Perth prison, where she went on hunger strike. She then suffered several days of cruel force-feeding, first orally, then by all accounts brutally through the rectum. In a statement to a newspaper, Fanny reported that a nurse had tried to force feed her vaginally. (Proteins can be absorbed via this route, but it would have been very slow and painful.)

Her brother, Captain Parker, managed to intervene and she was sent to a nursing home in Edinburgh, bruised and battered and apparently near collapse. Fanny wrote a report of her account in 1914, *Votes for Women*, which is not easy reading (see Scottish national archives).

At the start of the First World War she became part of the Women's Army Auxiliary Corps and went on to receive an OBE. She died at the age of 49 in France.

Women over 21 did not get the vote until 1928 so sadly for Fanny, she only saw some way to justice for women voters when certain women over the age of 30 gained the vote in 1918.

Lila Clunas (1876-1968). Although born in Glasgow, Lila trained as a teacher in Fife, and then went on to teach at Dundee Brown Street Public School. She became involved with the WSPU in 1906, and was secretary to the WFL along with her two sisters Elsie and Jessie. She often wrote letters to the press in favour of the women's vote. One such letter was quoted in the *Advertiser* of 1913: 'In this country in the past men have defied the law, and now their names are revered.'

Lila was thrown out of a meeting held by Dundee MP Winston Churchill in the summer of 1908 for bombarding him with questions. She felt this afternoon meeting was an insult to women, especially working-class females as they were at work or at home

Scottish Womens Freedom League. (Courtesy of LSE Library)

looking after children. Only 'ladies of leisure' were really free to attend the meeting.

Arrested in 1909 when she attempted to give a petition to Prime Minister Asquith, she was sentenced to three weeks in Holloway Prison, but was released early due to clemency. She was elected a Labour Party town councillor in 1943, and served until she was 88.

Lila continued to live in Broughty Ferry, Dundee, with her sister Elsie.

Florence Horsburgh (1889-1969). Although born in Edinburgh, she was to make her mark as the first female MP in Dundee, and represented the city in Westminster from 1931-1945.

Florence took over in 1931 from MP **Edwin Scrymgeour**, Scottish Prohibition Party, Dundee, as it has been argued that he may have only been voted in to oust Winston Churchill, who was opposed to women's votes. As Dundee had a large population of women breadwinners, it appears the feminist factor had worked against Churchill.

Although not a suffragette/suffragist Florence achieved many goals in her work as a Conservative MP, so it is for that reason she is

Suffragette postcard parliamentary candidate. (Courtesy of LSE Library)

listed here. It is believed she did not specifically deal with women's issues, as she felt she (and other female MPs) would not be helping feminist issues if that was all they concentrated on. To her, all her constituents were important. By the time she was elected in 1931, women over 21 were voting anyway. She did however help in the preparation towards the National Health Service (NHS) and was instrumental in The Adoption of Children Regulations Act 1939.

Between 1939 and 1945 she was health minister and at this time was instructed to organise the National Association of Training Corps for Girls. In 1951, she became minister of education in Churchill's government, and this then became a cabinet post, of which she was the first female.

Jane Kelly.
(Courtesy
of great
granddaughter
Louise Milne)

Jane Kelly (3rd from right back row). (Courtesy of great granddaughter Louise Milne)

Jane Kelly (née Dewar) (1877-1970) was born in a tenement in Dundee. She left school at 14 and taught music lessons to children. According to her great-granddaughter, Louise Milne, she liked to read the classics and was a tough, clever woman who attended suffragist meetings. Jane was friends with **Florence Horsburgh** and often chaired her meetings.

She married printer James Kelly around 1898, and he treated her as an equal.

Louise feels the economic situation at the time dictated the feminism.

Margaret Scott-Murray was born in Dundee and married the artist David Scott-Murray. Margaret was a suffragette and her husband designed the banner for the Perth branch, which was embroidered by Margaret and fellow suffragettes. Her great niece, Jean Bennet, recalls how in later years the banner was mounted on blue fabric and used as a room divider in the long drawing room of the family home in Scone.

Margaret
Scott-Murray.
(Courtesy of
family members
Niall and
Jean Bennett)

Jean remembers her great aunt as a small woman, and her mother saying how she could not imagine her as a militant suffragette.

The banner is now preserved in Perth Museum.

Marchioness of Tullibardine (later Duchess of Atholl) (1874-1960). Although born in Edinburgh, the duchess was well-known for her views on anti-suffrage. She became joint vice-president of the Anti-Suffrage League, Dundee Branch, in 1913.

She was involved in the Highlands and Islands Medical Service and was also vice-president of the Girls Public Day School Trust. She was the first woman in Scotland to be elected into parliament, in 1923, despite her views on abstaining from giving enfranchisement to women. In 1924 she argued 'there is no widespread desire for suffrage, and the suffragettes had become too militant'. A comment that outraged her fellow MP Nancy Astor, who saw her as 'Canute trying to keep the waves back'. The duchess was to remain an MP until 1938.

Katherine Macpherson lived in Charlotte Street, Perth. She was a WFL convenor and secretary for the organisation.

Although in Scotland women weren't admitted to universities before 1892, Katherine secured a Ladies Literate in Arts (LLA). Some females who wanted further education took this route, which meant they did not attend universities but took the courses through correspondence or attending classes that were not at a university. To obtain the relevant LLA certificate, Scottish ladies had to attend a university-approved centre, which may or may not have been in Scotland.

A mother of three and also a trained teacher, Katherine became more involved in suffrage, according to Leah Leneman's book, from 1913 onwards.

Victoria Drummond (1894-1978). Although not directly involved in suffrage (as far as research has shown), Victoria was born in Errol, Perthshire, and led a privileged life, being the daughter of wealthy parents. Her godmother was Queen Victoria.

However, Victoria Drummond, aged 20, took an apprenticeship as an engineer in Northern Garage, Perthshire, and then went onto work at a shipyard in Dundee. She passed several engineers' exams and worked on many ships over the years. She was awarded an MBE (Member of the British Empire) by King George V for her seagoing efforts in the Second World War.

She fought hard and eventually obtained a chief engineer's post. It appears very often she was overlooked (possibly due to the fact she was a woman in what was seen, back then, as a male-led job).

So although a suffragette, she was the first female member of the Institute of Marine Engineers and appears, despite discrimination, to have led the way forward for other females in this field.

CHAPTER FOUR

Aberdeen

Brief history

The name 'Aberdeen' probably comes from the Celtic word 'Aber', meaning river mouth, which is apt for the city as it lies between the rivers Dee and Don. Its history dates back 8,000 years. Industry in areas such as linen, wool, jute, and textiles gave employment to many Aberdonians. Whaling, shipbuilding, and paper-making were also part of the people of Aberdeen's working life.

However, the city has been well-known since the late 1960s for the discovery of North Sea crude oil. With an estimated half-a-million workers in the industry, mainly from Aberdeen, the area is often known as the European oil capital. Aberdeen's harbour saw modernisation around this time.

The city is Scotland's third most populated area. The motto for the city is Bon Accord, which is French for 'good agreement', and this is generally thought to have been credited to Robert the Bruce.

Historical population of Aberdeen

1851	Males = 34,694	Females = 43,185
1881	Males = 50,886	Females = 59,585
1911	Males = 82,525	Females = 97,550
1921	Males = 76,384	Females = 90,345
1951	Males = 87,826	Females = 103,174
1991	Males = 98,074	Females = 106,174
2011	Males = 110,122	Females = 112,671
2015	Males = 114,414	Females = 115,936

(a Vision of Britain timeline)

Of three paper mills in Aberdeen, only one now survives, Stoneywood Paper Mill, which opened in 1710. Women were employed in the paper mills, but it seems (from research photos) that they were not allowed to control the machines.

Grey granite was sourced in Aberdeenshire, and this was used in the building of the Houses of Parliament and Waterloo Bridge.

A popular modern-day feminist and well-known singer, Annie Lennox, was born in Aberdeen. In 2016 she was awarded the Livingstone Medal for services to AIDS recognition, and for her fight for women's rights. This was given by the Royal Scottish Geographical Society.

Working life

Back in the mid-nineteenth century, Aberdeen held auction markets and had wholesale butchers for the use of farmers in the area. It was cheaper to use family rather than pay wages to staff, so many of the single daughters (and sons) were relied on to help. However, by 1900 many of the female (and male) offspring wanted an education in order to eventually run their own farms. If female servants were employed on larger established farms, they were under the jurisdiction of the farmer's wife.

In the early to mid-nineteenth century, merchant manufacturers such as James Hadden often sent raw materials to cottar women (usually single or widowed females employed directly by an employer) for them to knit stockings at home, and then prices were agreed between the two on the finished article. However, females could earn more working at the textile factories that started to spring up. James Hadden took over a woollen mill in 1830 at Garlogie, where carpets were made as well as stockings and mittens, and wool was spun, with local women buying direct from the mill to knit for their families.

The company, it appears, looked after their employees with cottages to house some of them, and schooling for the children.

From the mid-1800s, children could only work just over six hours, and women up to twelve hours per day.

Supervisory and skilled posts at the mills were often given to the men and in other cities some mill owners dismissed females when they married. In Aberdeen, some of these women were kept on to teach others their skills.

As with many of the linen mills (and jute mills in Dundee), the wet spinning departments were not great areas to work in. Health was quite often affected, with respiratory illnesses taking their toll. The female workers liked to sing and chat to keep up morale, but in turn they were fined in many of the textile mills. A long working day and wage reductions at Broadfield Mill led to a strike in 1834.

It seems other girls came forward at this time from Banner Mill with many a tale of woe on the conditions they worked under and the strict discipline they endured. One girl had a splinter in her foot, two others helped her to remove it and they were all fined 6d (2½ pence).

According to Esther Breitenbach's book on Scottish Women, at Banner Mill the wages were paid wrongly to some of the women, and the action was rectified. But the girls wrongly paid were all fined 6d each, although not their fault.

In 1861, in Aberdeen there were 200 female teachers, but domestic service was still a large employer of women, especially from rural areas. In 1861, there were a reported 4,000 domestic women servants.

A large area of employment for Aberdeen women was in the fishing industry from the late 1800s to the early 1900s. The girls were employed on the boats to travel to various ports. Their task was to gut, salt and barrel the herring. The *Aberdeen Journal* of 1905 reported that 2,600 women worked gutting and salting fish in the city. However, conditions for the fish girls were pretty dire, and the Trades Council attempted to get these conditions improved. In 1913, the fish women successfully came out on strike for an increase in wages.

Aberdeen is well-known recently for its oil. However, these roles in oil favoured men rather than women, and it appears middle class rather than working class.

Industries such as soap and candle making employed a large section of women in their factories for stacking and wrapping soap bars and candles.

Aberdeen employed women in many trades such as tin factories, Hays lemonade factory, comb works and, from the late 1800s onwards, steam laundries gave women more employment, washing and ironing other people's linen. Some females, such as Mrs Green, Mrs Smith and Mrs Strachan, and all homeworkers in different parts of the city set up their own smaller businesses and appeared to do well. It was all hard work and could cause serious illnesses. But it gave the women flexibility in their working life.

The Aberdeen Ladies Union (ABL) was formed in 1883, aiming for the welfare of working women/girls in the area by raising moral standards within a Christian atmosphere. Some girls from rural areas were housed by ABL while undertaking domestic training. Unemployed women who could knit and sew were given work by the Ladies Working Society. This work was then sold by the Repository for Female Industry.

According to statistics from Vision of Britain by Aberdeen City, textile manufacturing data from 1951 showed that this was still the largest employment of females in the city centre. The 1971 data shows food and drink as the biggest employers.

In 1908, the National Union of Women Workers held its conference in Aberdeen on 13, 14 and 15 October. Some women in the 1800s and 1900s (and arguably well before that period) were not prepared to 'put up and shut up'. They stood up for what they believed was right, whether it be working conditions or poor or unequal pay.

Health & welfare

As with many cities, overcrowding and poor sanitation in the nineteenth century led to many diseases. In the late 1800s it was discovered that smallpox was often found in women who worked in the laundries, because they dealt with soiled linen. This was one of the ways the disease spread. The women carried the disease which then spread onwards. According to *The Lancet* in 1877, scarlet fever and tuberculosis were also rife in this area of women's work. A temporary smallpox hospital was opened in Mountbody, in a factory.

Because of these diseases, a bill was submitted to parliament which would have kept women from working in laundries within the first month of having a baby. This would have meant lost profits for business owners but wasn't passed into law.

Another infliction for women in the laundries was 'washer man's itch' (note man, not woman), which was a fungal infection due to the wet heat they had to deal with.

In 1903, Aberdeen appointed the first female health visitor, but her title then was sanitary inspector.

The spread of poliomyelitis occurred in the late 1800s after the corporation baths were opened for the 'great unwashed'. Many used the facilities, hence the spread of the disease through ingesting contaminated water.

Epidemics spread in the mid-1800s and 1900s similar to other Scottish cities with cholera, typhoid, typhus and measles. However, in 1964 typhus broke out again in Aberdeen due to contaminated corned beef and factories were forced to close. Many able-bodied female factory workers couldn't claim poor relief and were forced to turn to prostitution.

Poverty in all areas of Scotland (and England) was very evident. In Aberdeen in the mid-1800s, just over two per cent of the city's population was poverty stricken. Money for day-to-day living had to be earned somewhere.

The Industrial Reformatory and Asylum was open for girls of 'bad habits' in the mid-1800s. Many were neglected and destitute, so they were given shelter and were trained for domestic or laundry service.

Many organisations sprung up with the intention of giving help to the poor and unemployed. For women there were often specific groups to help them. This in turn would keep them off the streets and earning a little money to survive.

A leading campaigner for health improvements in Aberdeen was **Lady Matilda (May) Baird** (1901-1983). She undertook her medical training in Glasgow, but moved with her husband, Sir Dugald Baird, a doctor, in 1936 to Aberdeen. She became the first chairwoman of the North East Regional Hospital Board in

1947, on which she served nearly twenty years. She was also chair of Aberdeen's Public Health Committee from 1938 to 1954.

Dr Mary Esslemont (1891-1984), another champion lady who was born in Aberdeen and obtained her medical degree in 1923, was actively involved in work with the poor and under-privileged, and was also know for supporting women's rights.

Education

Education in Aberdeen in the early 1800s seemed to focus more on boys' education, certainly like most cities where parents on lower incomes sent their girls (and boys) out to earn a living. Sometimes the mills, such as Gordon's Mill, employed a teacher to teach the children, boys and girls, the 3Rs. More often than not the poorer families needed the children to work in order to bring in money for food. Aberdeen had about fifty dame schools.

Two-thirds of girls worked at various mills. A census taken at Granholm Mill in the 1800s showed that only twenty-eight per cent of these could read and write, some either one or the other, and another twenty-seven per cent could do neither. After a full day's work at the mill, even if some of the girls did attend education, they were often so tired from work they fell asleep.

Church-assisted schools helped the destitute and poorer classes. Both sexes were taught the 3Rs, but again females were generally taught about domestic training while males were even taught foreign languages. Females were clearly regarded as second-class citizens.

In the 1800s, schools of industry were formed. The Aberdeen Female Schools of Industry in 1881 had 108 female students ranging from age 6 to 19. Most of these schools aimed at keeping females off the streets, away from begging and suchlike, with a view to educating and training for domestic or industry work.

After the introduction of The Education (Scotland) Act of 1872, both male and female children, aged 5 to 13, were required to receive basic education.

The Ladies Educational Association was set up in the nineteenth century, with the aim of making it possible to obtain higher education for females. The Aberdeen branch was formed and, in 1881, various lectures were advertised and taught to women. These included languages, literature, geography and many other subjects. The association survived for seven years but closed in 1886 after student numbers diminished. However, 1892 was the turning point when the doors were opened for females to study. Two years later, twenty women started their courses, and six years on saw the first four women graduate in the arts. In 1899, a quarter of the student population at the university were female.

The university saw its first female lecturer in Humanity (Latin) appointed in 1903. However, the title of lecturer was not bestowed until 1906. In 1925, a women's union was set up there, and it appears that even in the 1930s women were still not truly represented at the university.

Suffrage, politics, women and notable men

Various meetings occurred in the 1900s in Aberdeen. English suffragettes Adela Pankhurst and Helen Fraser (the first Scottish WSPU organiser in 1906) campaigned in 1907 at the Aberdeen South by-elections. In 1908, Christabel Pankhurst (Adela's sister) spoke publicly at a meeting, of which there was much controversy. Many of the women in Aberdeen were staunch Liberal. However, Mrs Allan, honorary secretary, and Mrs Black, president, of the Women's Liberal Association (WLA) in Aberdeen seemed to be condemned for attending a suffrage meeting. They hit back, commenting their 'record of active support for the Liberal party was second to none, but this is a woman's question, and we must be loyal to our womanhood'.

In November 1912, Reverend Forbes Jackson was attacked at Aberdeen station by Emily Wilding Davison, who mistook him for David Lloyd George, Chancellor of the Exchequer. She hit the minister with a whip. At the time the chancellor was holding a Liberal meeting in Aberdeen.

The attempted burning of Ashley Road School in 1913 hit the headlines, as it was supposedly set on fire by the suffragettes. A copy of *Suffragette* and other suffrage material were found nearby.

Dr Mary Esslemont (1891-1984) was born in Aberdeen. She was committed to women's rights and it is believed she was a suffragist.

Mary was on the negotiating committee and represented the National Women's Federation on the development of the NHS. However, in 1945, when a meeting was organised at the Cafe Royal to discuss the NHS, only a sixth of the negotiating members were invited. They were all male. Mary was not invited.

It was clear even in this period there was a lot of inequality amongst influential men with women in professions.

Aneurin Bevan, minister for health at the time and instrumental in the formation of the NHS, it seems had little regard for women in politics, or it appears independent women. It is argued in Marvin

Mary Esselemont. (Courtesy of the Wellcome Collection)

Rintala's book on the NHS that Bevan's failure to notice Mary wasn't at the negotiating meeting was no accident. Neither were there any nurses.

Mary was also active in The Scottish Convention of Women (SCOW), which was said to have had a part in the Scottish government culture.

Louisa Innes Lumsden (1840-1935) was a non-militant suffragist who was born in Aberdeen. She was one of the first of three women to study the classics and sat, unofficially, the Honours examination at Cambridge University. She was an innovator of female education, being the first headmistress of St Andrew's School.

In 1908, she became the president of the Aberdeen Suffrage Society, was vice president of the Scottish Churches League for Women's Suffrage, and a member of the executive committee of the Scottish Federation. She attended a huge gathering in 1913 with Chrystal Macmillan (from Edinburgh), making a speech at Hyde Park on behalf of the NUWSS. The *Dundee Advertiser* commented that it was a 'uniquely, impressive demonstration'.

In the autumn of that year, Louisa was a prominent speaker for the Scottish Federation of the NUWSS. She, along with Lady Betty Balfour, Lady Frances Balfour and Millicent Fawcett, spoke in all corners of Scotland. As far north as Wick and Orkney, down to North Berwick and across to Oban.

On a quirky note, Louisa had a horse-drawn caravan, called *Curlew*, built to transport Louisa and her dog from Aberdeen to Edinburgh. She willingly lent this to Helen Fraser in the summer of 1908 so that she could tour Scotland for the NUWSS.

May Pollock Grant (also known as **Marion Pollock**) (1856-1957) was born in Dundee but became well known in Aberdeen in 1912.

She, Fanny Parker (mentioned under Dundee), and Joyce Locke (from London), were found bundled in a pay box inside Aberdeen Music Hall. They were apparently lying in wait to disrupt David Lloyd George's meeting. They were found, arrested and given five days in prison having been found guilty of carrying small, explosive caps.

Caroline Phillips (1870-1956) was born in Kintore, Aberdeen. She became a journalist for the *Aberdeen Daily Journal* in 1900, a job not many women undertook in that period. She worked for the newspaper for twelve years and then went on to run the Station Hotel, Banchory, which her aunt left her. Although she covered suffrage events and often sent letters on the newspaper's headed paper, her employers were not entirely happy with her strong connection to the suffrage movement, and she was reprimanded by her bosses, who felt she needed to distance herself but still report on events. It appears this is something Caroline did not wholeheartedly do.

Caroline was honorary secretary for the Aberdeen WSPU for two years, from 1907 to 1909, although some conflict appears to have occurred between her and the Pankhurst family.

She reported on the 'goings on' of the suffragettes in the *Aberdeen Daily Journal* and she corresponded with Emmeline and her daughter Christabel during the spring of 1907, when they were trying to arrange meetings in Aberdeen. There appear to have been tensions in the WSPU later that year as a few members were not happy with Mrs Pankhurst and the fierce militant tactics her group employed. Several members left, such as Teresa Billington-Greig, and the Women's Freedom League was formed. Aberdeen suffrage had its fair share of disturbance.

When Asquith was due to speak at the music hall, there was talk of a possible suffragette disruption, and it appears Caroline took it upon herself to write to the president of the WLA privately to state, 'our Aberdeen WSPU are in the mood to leave him severely alone!'

Caroline, although honorary secretary to the WSPU, had tried to engage with the Liberal ladies in Aberdeen again and in 1908 she invited Mrs Black and Mrs Allan, honorary secretary of the group, to sit on the stage with Christabel Pankhurst. It was hoped that militants and non-militants at that time could work together in anticipation of votes for women.

Angry protests from both sides occurred. In the backlash, both Mrs Black and Mrs Allan resigned from their positions at the WLA.

Caroline's place in the Aberdeen WSPU had started to look uncertain since the music hall incident and, despite correspondence, mainly with Christabel, her position as honorary secretary of the Aberdeen WSPU was terminated by a curt telegram in January 1909. She was informed that Sylvia Pankhurst would assume charge of the local work. In fact, the branch was closed and members were transferred to the national organisation. Caroline was not mentioned one way or another then, until a meeting of July 1909 in Union Street, when she and several others including Sylvia Pankhurst were the subject of much bitterness from members of the group. The president, Lady Agnes Ramsay, is also reported as adding her criticism.

The fact that Caroline was not there to defend herself was a 'pretty poor show', and it would seem that the group, local and national, had developed a good deal of in-house squabbling.

It appears that Caroline, although still reporting at the newspaper, did not attend any further meetings. She wrote to her friend Agnes McRobbie: 'They can have my scalp, as long as the movement doesn't suffer.'

Teresa Billington-Greig (1877-1964). Although born in England, Teresa's connection to Scotland began in 1906 when she was sent by the WSPU to organise a Scottish branch. While there she married Scotsman Frederick Lewis Greig.

She spoke at many meetings, including the Aberdeen by-election where Liberal women's views were contended, even if some had supported women's suffrage.

In 1907, she was secretary of the Scottish council of the WSPU, but in October she left to form the WFL. She appears to have been popular in Scotland and was a suffragist not a suffragette, and this may have irritated the Pankhursts. Teresa was not keen on some of the militant tactics, hence Emmeline and Christabel took over as mentioned previously.

She was part of the WFL until 1910, when it seems their organisation started to become militant. When the Conciliation Bill did not happen due to the election, she resigned.

During the period before and after she this she was an avid writer and she published many articles on equal rights and feminism

VOTES FOR WOMEN.

MRS. T. BILLINGTON-GREIG.
HON. ORGANISING SEC. WOMEN'S FREEDOM LEAGUE.
1, ROBERT STREET. ADELPHI. LONDON. W.C.

PHOTO BRINKLEY & SO
GLASGOW

Teresa
Billington-
Greig.
(Courtesy of
LSE Library)

including one piece entitled *The Militant Suffrage Movement*. According to the Working Class Movement Library, Teresa wrote and received income from *New Age* and *The Contemporary Review* publications. She was also a freelance speaker. With all the many women and organisations supporting their crusade, the Pankhurst family appears to have wanted control and to keep militant tactics strong, whatever the cost.

Ishbel Hamilton-Gordon (Marchioness of Aberdeen) (1857-1939) was born in London. She moved to Aberdeen at the age of 20 when she wed John Hamilton-Gordon, 1st Marquess of Aberdeen and Temair.

Ishbel had a good education and could have furthered her learning, but her father was of the opinion that university was not an option for females. She was a strong supporter of women's views and their rights.

Ishbel and her husband lived in Haddo House, Aberdeen (now a National Trust property), and London. Her husband was a Liberal and a member of the House of Lords. She spent some time in Canada due to her husband's work and established branches of national

Ishbel of
Aberdeenshire.
(Courtesy of
Lord Aberdeen)

Ishbel Countess of Aberdeen. (Courtesy of The 7th Marquess of Aberdeen & Temair)

women's councils there. She was also involved in the NHS in Ireland, again living there for a while due to Lord Aberdeen's work. She established the Onwards & Upwards Association for young women in rural areas. The incentive was to keep them in rural employment while achieving learning through postal courses on various subjects.

In 1893, she was the first president of the International Council of Women. She was also president of the Women's Liberal Federation from 1893 to 1894 and 1902 to 1906.

According to Leah Leneman's book, Ishbel was also vice-president of both NUWSS and Glasgow and West Association of Women's Suffrage. However, no further evidence has been found of this, and her great grandson, the current Lord Aberdeen, is not aware of her being involved in either organisation, despite her commitment to furthering females' education.

Lilias Mitchell (1884-1940) was born in Leith, Scotland. She attended various suffrage meetings with her mother and joined the WSPU in 1907, aged 23. She said she felt completely lifted out of herself when listening to Emmeline Pankhurst at the meeting.

She became organiser of the Aberdeen WSPU branch in 1911, her predecessor being English women Ada Flatman, who had in fact replaced Caroline Phillips. It seems Lilias was unaware that an Aberdeen branch existed.

The following year saw her take part in a 200-plus contingent of women in London, smashing shop windows. Kensington High Street was the domain of the Scottish suffragettes. She and others were arrested and imprisoned in Holloway. Lilias resisted food, but swallowed some during a struggle. Due to a weakened heart from previous scarlet fever, she had worried about the effect of force-feeding, albeit she wielded a hammer to smash windows with some force.

After her four-month stay in prison and with her mother's support, she returned to Scotland.

In September 1912, she was back in England with another suffragette, replacing flags at Balmoral Golf Course with messages about force-feeding and votes for women. This was apparently aimed at politicians who were in the vicinity.

Back in the north of Scotland, at Dornoch Golf Course the same year, she was up to mischief again, this time with English suffragette Elsie Howie. They attacked Prime Minister Asquith, and Home Secretary Reginald McKenna.

Time after this was spent in the organisation of WSPUs in Birmingham and Newcastle. She was also involved in a home-made bomb at a Birmingham railway station.

After 1918, she was involved with the YWCA and Citizens Advice Bureau, both in Edinburgh.

Unfortunately, her weakened heart led to her early death aged 56.

Helen Ogston's father was an Aberdeen professor and she obtained a BSc at St Andrews University. Helen's claim to fame with the suffrage cause was her attendance at a meeting at the Albert Hall in London in December 1908.

David Lloyd George in London. (Courtesy of LSE Library)

David Lloyd George, Chancellor of the Exchequer, was to speak and he had (it seems) promised he would 'strenuously oppose any measure failing to give votes to the working man's wife'. He had told the WLF by letter that he would bring up the subject of votes for women at the Albert Hall meeting. This he did not do. Did he have any intention of doing so? If he did, was it because heckling women had thrown off their clothing to reveal prison garments in protest of women suffrage prisoners?

Helen stood up from her place on the second level and was shouting loudly. She was about to be manhandled by the male stewards, but had secretly hidden a dog whip in her clothes, with which she hit them. This made headlines around the world.

The Illustrated London News on 12 December 1908 printed a sketch of her hitting the men. She argued that she was frightened of being attacked by the men and that was why she had taken the whip. According to Sylvia Pankhurst's book *The Suffragette Movement: an intimate account of persons and ideal,* Ms Pankhurst asked Helen to leave the whip behind for fear of making matters worse. Sylvia was called away and obviously Ms Ogston did take the whip with her.

In the book, Sylvia reports that Helen said she was struck in the chest, had a cigarette stubbed out on her wrist, and several of the men struck her down. 'I could not endure it,' she had said.

Sylvia Pankhurst spoke in Aberdeen 1909 image. (Courtesy of LSE Library)

Sylvia goes on to say that afterwards, Helen received a 'splendid reception' in Aberdeen.

Research has shown that often the women at these type of events were dealt with roughly. Helen apparently said: 'In the melee I hit out at one of the men who was behaving brutally.'

Sylvia declared this is what happened when the women were just trying to ask a question of the chancellor.

Why did the men at this event, and other events like it, feel this was a justified action on the women? Were the women who used militant action (not particularly at this event) justified in their sometimes harsh actions? Everyone will make their own judgement.

In 1909, Helen and her sister Constance were on the receiving end of harsh criticism by the Aberdeen WSPU.

Isabella Fyvie Mayo (1843-1914) had Scottish parents but was born in London. Her childhood had been cut short when her father died leaving the family with debts. So she was obliged to seek work in a law firm.

At the age of 27, she married John Mayo, a lawyer in London. Unfortunately, the marriage was short-lived as he died seven years later. Isabel and her son moved back to Aberdeen. She had been writing and over the years penned many novels, sometimes under the name of Edward Garrett. Much of her work featured strong women who could match their male counterparts.

She was involved with Aberdeen Ladies Educational Association as their secretary in 1881. In 1894, she was elected to the Aberdeen school board. She was also a candidate for the Labour Party.

According to a book by James D. Hunt, Isabella although a supporter of women's suffrage, believed that the vote was more for tax-paying women rather than all women, as not all men were given

Christabel Pankhurst. (Courtesy of LSE Library)

the vote at that time. It appears she did not like some of the militant tactics, as with so many other women wanting enfranchisement but not the violence. So she was a suffragist.

In 1907, she was a speaker at an Aberdeen WSPU meeting and criticised another group, the Aberdeen Women's Suffrage Society, saying they were 'ineffectual'. However, rifts were occurring in this local branch of the WSPU and Mrs Pankhurst overruled Mrs Mayo on several occasions.

Christabel Pankhurst wrote to Caroline Phillips in November 1907, saying: 'Mrs Mayo, not long ago said she would leave the union, it is a great pity she did not keep her word.'

Mrs Mayo features in the Aberdeen Heritage Woman's Trail.

John Duguid Milne (1822-1889) was a campaigner for women's rights. He was Aberdeen's city assessor.

In the mid-1800s, he wrote the book *The Industrial and Social Position of Women*, in which he argued about the meaningful employment of women in order to give them a purpose. The original book was published anonymously, but in 1870 he revised the book, and published it under his own name.

He was instrumental in forming the Aberdeen Ladies Educational Association and, as a member of the university council, often supported women's claims for education.

James Murray (1850-1932) held the post of East Aberdeenshire Liberal MP. It was well known that Mr Murray was in support of women's suffrage.

Emmeline Pankhurst corresponded with journalist and suffragist Caroline Phillips in May 1907, enquiring about a meeting that Mr Murray would be holding with a view to discussing enfranchisement. Mr Asquith was invited to the music hall meeting and, as mentioned previously, there was a great deal of furore going on. However, it seems Mrs Pankhurst and her daughter were grateful to Mr Murray, and letters seem to have flown between Caroline Phillips, Lady Ramsey and Helen Fraser praising Mr Murray's support.

CHAPTER FIVE

Stirling and surrounding areas

Brief history

Stirling was given city status by Queen Elizabeth II in her golden jubilee year, 2002. The name Stirling is believed to come from the word 'striveling', meaning place of strife. Carvings can be found in Kings' Park dating back to the Stone Age.

The city is in central Scotland, bordering the Lowlands and the Highlands, with the picturesque Ochil Hills surrounding the area.

Standing proud is Stirling Castle, built originally in the thirteenth century of timber, but then rebuilt in stone. The castle along with the city has seen many battles over the years. William Wallace, Robert the Bruce and Bonnie Prince Charlie have all had parts to play in the area. Mary Queen of Scots lived here and her son, King James VI of Scotland (James I of England), was crowned here.

Several battles with the English saw Stirling Castle change hands several times and, in the seventeenth century, the king spent most of his time in England. Some historians feel that at the time the area was unimportant.

A census shows in the early eighteenth century that the population was only 4,000, but by 1821 it had grown to 7,333. The city was once a bustling inland port with the River Forth flowing through. It dealt with foreign trade such as tea from India and timber from the Baltic, bringing wealth and important influence to the area. Plagues in the early and mid-1600s depleted the population with over 600,000 deaths.

Cholera was rife in the 1800s with, again, more deaths. Sanitation was not good, hence the diseases that followed. Almshouses were built to help the poor, and local asylums housed many who possibly were not meant to be there.

Several Stirling women paved the way for equality.

Working life

Scotland as a whole had a great deal of textile industry, spinning and wool-makers. Domestic service also played a part in many women's lives in Stirling and the surrounding areas. Coal was needed to make boilers work, creating steam for powering looms. It was also used to power the trains that came to Stirling in the 1840s.

Coal-mining was a big industry and it appears that the Redding Colliery, Stirlingshire, owned by the Duke of Hamilton back in the mid-1800s, employed more than a quarter of the workforce as women.

The Scottish Mining website contains accounts from many women and children who worked in the mines. One young lass stated: 'It is quite our own will, but make more money by it.'

Often this was the only employment option for some women in the early nineteenth century, and women and children were usually paid less than the men, yet they still worked eleven or twelve hours a day.

In the Bantaskine and Callendar Colliery, in Falkirk, surrounding Stirling, owner John Wilson was concerned for his colliers' welfare. He said: 'I tried to restrict females from working, but would lose some of my best colliers.' He did make sure that they only worked in one mine.

Times were hard for everyone. They had to work to eat, but even so, wages varied greatly from 10d per day to 27 shillings per week. Women appear to have been paid less than the men for the same number of hours worked. An 1878 Act of Parliament stated women and children had to work above ground in mines.

Cotton spinning and weaving was a large employer of low-skilled women who were poorly paid in most instances, but obviously some work was better than no work. Weaving in Scotland as a whole was predominantly undertaken by women. However, in the 1901 census, only eight per cent of Stirling women were employed in mills, although other textile manufacturers sprung up in the surrounding areas. Half of the working women of Stirling were employed in Clackmannan.

Lennox Mill at Compsie had 135 women working at their calico printing mill. The wages were allegedly better than most, at approximately 5-6 shillings per week. They were often tasked with pencilling colour onto the fabrics and were called 'colourers'.

There were about nine yarn-spinning and woollen mills in the 1800s in Stirling, Alva and Bannockburn, with more than 600 women employed. There were several other mills dotted about the surrounding areas, such as the Old Kinbuck Mill (nineteenth century) powered by the Allan Water River.

The women of Tillicoutry Mill even then showed their resilience. When a mill-dam was introduced by the owners, taking away some of the women's work, the headstrong females demolished the dam using spades, pickaxes and other 'to hand' tools.

Forty per cent of all women in Stirling in the early 1900s were employed in domestic service, so it was generally thought that, due to the isolation of the work, no organisation happened between the women. The work was often lonely and long hours, and it appears equal pay was not the 'order of the day'.

In some domestic work the women did not get paid at regular intervals. It could be as long as six months before they received their wages. In most instances, they at least had a roof over their heads.

From accounts in *Five Bob a Week,* a Stirling women's work publication that details accounts from local working women between 1900-1950, one lady, Mrs N., worked as a teenager in a hotel in the early 1920s and, by her own admission, you were 'nothing more than a skivvy'. She went on to say: 'There was no such thing as hours ... you just worked.'

The rubber works in Stirling provided many women with jobs in the early 1900s, making chamber pots, gloves, hot water bottles and suchlike. At age 21, the women were paid the highest amount of £28 and were allowed one week's unpaid holiday a year.

Howietoun Fisheries just outside Stirling also employed women in the late 1800s. James Maitland, who ran the fishery, wrote in his book: 'A trained woman was able to dress ten boxes in an hour

Howietoun Fisheries 1925. (Courtesy Stirling University Archives)

without damage to the fish ova.' (Fish eggs were dressed into rows with a quill feather.) He said that the men at the establishment were too heavy-handed do this. His daughter Mary took over the business when both her parents died. Women obviously had their uses.

With the First World War upon Stirling, many domestic jobs were on the decline as women took up some of the posts left by the men who had gone to war. Pit work, post office workers, some worked in the Royal Mechanical and Engineers, which maintained army supplies. There was also a secret aircraft factory in Alloa where seamstresses were employed to cover the wings of Sopwith Camel biplanes with linen.

Local resident Andrew Wood from Dunfermline remembers his aunt, **Margaret (Peggy) Honeyman**, and mother, **Elizabeth Honeyman**, working in the factory. It appears the total workforce was thirty-three and thirteen women were employed here in 1916. By all accounts the workers were looked after well. The unskilled women who worked in what was called the dope area were only

WW1 Women posties in Bridge of Allan 1914. (Courtesy Stirling University Archives)

allowed to remain working there for short periods (probably twenty minutes), and then had to go outside.

The dope area was where the women used very strong plasticised lacquer to tighten and make waterproof the linen used on the wings of the Sopwith Camel planes. Due to the toxic nature, it could have the effect of someone sniffing glue if exposed for too long, and could make the women ill. The substance was eventually banned.

It would appear at this particular workplace the welfare of women workers (and the men) was foremost. There was a factory inspector and women also had the backing of the National Federation for Women Workers (founded by Mary Macarthur from Glasgow.).

One worker, Bella Mackinson, became a welfare officer for the girls in every department. The following extract (kindly sent by her granddaughter Beth) demonstrates the respect and care for female workers that the Caudron Aerodrome management showed them:

> We were treated with full respect from the directors, in their office for meetings, I was the only woman and I was given a chair. We received wages according to the rules, and ten minutes tea break in the morning and afternoon.

In the Second World War there were nearly 23,000 women working for LMS Railways. Sadly, after the war, as unemployment was high, returning men took precedence over women for jobs.

Caudron Aircraft factory, Peggy Honeyman 2nd row, 6th from left. (Courtesy of Alloa Library Archive)

Whatever employment women sought in those early years in history, it is clear:

a) Needs must was an important factor early on, just living day-to-day for a great deal of women.
b) In many of the jobs women took on, a sing-song was high on the agenda, and they liked to chat. It would appear that, unfortunately, domestic work did not lend its hand to this very often, as it was quite solitary work.
c) Although some employment, such as pit working, did not have unions or similar for women, there was, in most cases, a strong, camaraderie among the females. They looked out for one another.

In the late 1800s, women did not appear to have any trade unions to improve or maintain their working situations. The Scottish Council of Women's Trades (SCWT) may have infiltrated Stirling and surrounding areas, suggesting the organisation of women workers. Some unions were formed such as the Tillicoutry Textile workers union, which is believed accepted women workers.

Heath & welfare

Stirling in the early nineteenth century was cramped and dirty and the sanitation was badly lacking. Poorhouses sprung up, as did asylums. Poor relief was given to at least eight per cent of Stirling's population.

In 1881, it was documented at the Combination Poorhouse that there were ninety-six inmates, forty-four of whom females (five under 16 years of age).

Diseases such as cholera and typhoid were rife. There was a high infant mortality rate. Cholera struck several times in Stirling, in 1832, 1848 and 1853, killing a great many people. Only the rich could afford doctors. The poor had to use the public dispensary that sometimes had one doctor.

Cowane's hospital, which was established in the mid-1600s, became a cholera isolation unit. In 1837, typhus and influenza caused the death of many others. Things had to change.

At least when the 1832 Reform Act came into force, although ordinary men and women were still not allowed to vote (only those who owned or rented property at £10), the way was paved for improvements in local services.

In Larbert stood the Old Stirling Lunatic Asylum (now Bellsdyke Hospital). It opened to patients in 1869 and closed in 1997. According to archived material in Stirling University, a great number of patients admitted to the asylum were women

Sub-acute puerperal insanity was a condition affecting mothers mentally post-childbirth and was a common ailment listed. One report in the casebooks notes Mrs F. aged 24, who had been in domestic service, who had whisky poured down her throat to calm her down. This ended in a cataleptic seizure, which in turn ended in her death. Other women were put into the asylum with reasons documented as sub-acute adolescent, alcoholism, epilepsy, and so on. Were women placed in these asylums because they had become 'inconvenient' to their husbands or family?

One housewife in Stirling Asylum felt people were trying to poison her and said that her husband was bad. She died at the age of 32, a month after admission, with the post-mortem concluding she had 'acute softening of the brain'.

What does this have to do with female suffrage and the vote for women? Fundamentally, it was a stepping stone for women to stand up to the authorities and voice their concerns over issues that were important.

Drink in the nineteenth century played a part in many peoples lives, which in turn affected health, family life, and caused an increase in crime. The Stirling Board of Health even issued posters warning of excessive alcohol consumption leading to diseases and crime. A temperance society was formed in 1831 in Stirling in order to stop people drinking spirits and limit wine and beer.

Mrs **Elizabeth Maclean** was a member of the local temperance society, she was a middle-class lady keen to help others. An active member of the Stirling Female Society for the Relief of Aged and Indigent Women, she was probably also well aware of the plight of working women in the burgh.

The temperance movement involved women who were concerned about social issues and were campaigning in politics. Respectable women who wanted to see moral improvement joined the temperance societies, but like Mrs Maclean, their causes further developed to suffrage.

A 1913 Temperance (Scotland) Act allowed only eligible electorate to vote on whether to make burghs alcohol-free. Due to the First World War, implementation of the act was delayed until 1920 when the results of the 1913 poll was finally enacted.

Sixteen women charged with prostitution were held in the cells of Stirling police station in 1854. Poverty, poor housing and a lack of substantial pay at their jobs were apparently to blame and prostitution was the only way to 'make ends meet.' According to Louise Settle's book *Sex for sale in Scotland*, many of these women came from poor backgrounds and were on low wages or unable to find work. So they worked as prostitutes in order to survive.

This kind of work brought about abuse and ill health. Many died young. Some were sent to asylums such as the Old Stirling Lunatic Asylum. Lock hospitals sprang up to treat women for venereal diseases. It appears women were originally the targets of propaganda on the spread of such diseases, and not the men who attended brothels or frequented the sex workers.

Doctor Elizabeth Rose was the founder of the first family planning clinic in Stirling.

Education

In the mid-1800s, child labour had increased to fifty-three per cent in the Clackmannanshire area had increased, according to W.W. Knox in *A history of Scottish People*. It would appear to some folk that educating girls 'was a waste of time'. Their future was mapped out for marriage and having children. As mentioned before, domestic service was the prevalent employment for many single lasses in the nineteenth century. The poorer classes had to send their children out to work rather than to school.

In Stirling there were several schools dating from the 1150s. These were run by the church. The old fee-paying high school was built in 1863 (on the site of the present Highland Hotel), but then moved site in the 1960s. Most headteachers appear to have been male, but that is not to say there were no female teachers. However, in 1849 the Ragged school was opened for destitute children, which was free. It began with boys only, but in 1850 girls were admitted. Although run by a male headteacher, there was a female matron on site. It seems girls were taught mainly domestic topics.

The first school boards were introduced in 1870, and then women were elected. It would appear many of these women were at the forefront of women's suffrage.

Two school mistresses were recorded in 1876/7 for the Ragged school, and then onwards as the headteachers changed they appear to have also been women. Salaries, however, did not reflect this. Male teachers between 1872 and 1900 were paid

£121-£145 per year, compared to women teachers who had an income of £62-£72 per year. Men argued that the women were not the main breadwinners.

Stirling was home to some private establishments for young ladies. Noted in *Stirling … The Royal Burgh* by Craig Muir, classes in deportment and manners were listed, along with special attractions of servants at dinner for the pupils. This ran alongside the usual curriculum.

Suffrage, politics, women and notable men

In the 1900s, suffrage was all about the vote for women as we know, but feminists had been around for much longer. Their aim was, and is, rights for women, including political, social, economic and personal. They campaigned for equal opportunities for women in professional and educational stakes.

Much is written in other publications about **Mary Wollstonecraft**, a British feminist in the eighteenth century. In 1792, aged 34, she wrote the book *Vindication in the Rights of Women*, declaring the rights of equality of women. This is likely to have paved the way for many continuing feminists in both the UK and further afield.

In Stirling, as with a lot of areas, suffrage was around but events seemed to have calmed down somewhat. Petitions were still being signed for the women's right to vote, but it would appear Stirling's town council in the mid-1870s did not respond to the Edinburgh Society's requests.

In 1892, the Scottish Co-operative Women's Guild was a working-class women's group interested in fundraising and covered various domestic ideas, but they gave women more insight into professions, skills and public speaking. Often these groups were interested in suffrage and political matters, which were discussed thoroughly at their meetings.

Of the middle-class women, the National Society for Women's Suffrage in Edinburgh requested a meeting in April 1871 to be held in Stirling.

Falkirk Suffragettes. (Courtesy of Falkirk Council Archives)

Miss Jane Taylour, who was secretary of the Galloway branch, spoke of suffrage following on from MP Jacob Bright's Bill, which had first and second readings in parliament in favour of women voters in burghs and counties, if they were householders and listed on the ratepayers list.

(It must be noted that Liberal MP Jacob Bright appears to have fought over several years in the House of Commons towards women getting the vote. From 1870 onwards, reading excerpts from Hansard, Jacob Bright and several other members of parliament tried in vain to get the votes for women.)

In 1873, Stirling held another suffrage meeting. Many men supported the women in their fight, even influential men such as bankers, men of the cloth, merchants and so on, spoke at these early meetings.

Jessie Hannah Craigen was among Stirling's suffragist speakers. She was from a working-class background, born in 1835. It is believed her father was a Scottish sailor and her mother an Italian actress. She spoke at countless suffrage movements around the country. In May 1875, at Stenhousemuir Cross near Stirling, she held a meeting of ironworkers and colliers, and in 1876 she held a meeting at Limerigg near Stirling. It appears many men attended some of her meetings as well as women.

Many felt that because of the 'bad laws', women were oppressed and a fair share of representation would be advisable for female workers. So although suffrage meetings began in the early 1900s in Stirling, it is fair to say that some women and women workers were already not happy with their lot. It was not just the middle-class ladies.

Janet (Jenny) McCallum. In Dunfermline, 23 miles from Stirling, was another working-class female, who worked in a local textile factory, Mathewson's. In 1908, she joined the Women's Freedom League in London after leaving her job, and due to her rioting outside the House of Commons was imprisoned in Holloway for twenty-eight days.

Many of the women who had previously been thrown out by police at Parliament Buildings, attempted to force their way in again, thus the arrest. Jenny and other suffragettes from England made the daily newspapers the following day in an article in *The Times* entitled *The Riot*.

Jenny McCallum(top right). (Courtesy of great niece Sheila Perry)

Christian Mclagan (1809-1901), another notable feminist in the area, was educated at home as a child. She later became, it is believed, the first female archaeologist. Her main interest was the brochs (prehistoric stone towers) of Scotland, and she went on to write several books. However, many thought her ideas eccentric. The idea of a woman interested and writing about such a subject! She was unable to obtain a fellowship of the Antiquities of Scotland, and was only made a lady associate.

A very determined woman, she sent her stone-rubbings to the British Museum instead. It appears she was a very feisty lady for her time, but also a compassionate one who promoted education and devoted time and money to clearing the slums in Stirling.

Jessie Yuille was another prominent woman in Stirling. As wife of the pastor of a Stirling Baptist church and secretary of the Baptist Union of Scotland, she became involved and lent her support to the local British Woman's Temperance Association. She was also leader in 1905 of the local WSPU in Stirling. She was an active member and leader of the Women's Auxiliary of the Baptist Union of Scotland and was involved in organising protests and demonstrations campaigning against wartime prohibition. So, although no stranger to objecting to what she believed was right, as a member of the church she probably would not have been united in the sometime violence that prevailed the suffragette movement.

Jane Grieson was an organiser for WSPU in Cambusbarron. She was a suffragette and activist for the Labour Party. Tom Johnston was a Labour MP who supported suffrage and wrote so in his newspaper *Forward*. Jane helped chair his meetings from 1918-1922, and during the mining disputes, this spirited woman ran a soup kitchen in Cambusbarron.

Helen Matthews (Graham) was born in Montrose, Angus. She was a suffragette who caused a stir in 1881 when she set up the first female football team, based in Stirling. They played their first match against English suffragettes in Edinburgh. At the women's second

WSPU postcard album 1911. (Courtesy of LSE Library)

match in Glasgow, a riot started due to the females wearing trousers while playing the match. Their team did win but caused controversy leading to the banning of women playing football in Scotland. Undeterred, they played under pseudonyms and often crossed into England to play. Mrs Graham's XI team was also recognised as having the first black female football player, Emma Clarke from Liverpool. She was apparently a neighbour of Mrs Graham and toured Scotland as a goalkeeper for the team.

Mrs Edmund Pullar from Bridge of Allan was president of the Stirling NUWSS in 1913, and her vice president was **Mrs Lambert-Brown** from Stirling.

An enthusiastic evening's meeting was held in the Bridge of Allan in April 1911, chaired by Mrs Pullar with speaker Mrs Chrystal Macmillan from Edinburgh (who was later to become a Liberal MP). An article in the *Stirling and Bridge of Allan Reporter* newspaper concluded that many women were present at the meeting with 'the mere men not conspicuous by their absence'.

The Stirling branch by 1914 had more than 100 women, and the Stirling Women's Unionist Association had well over 700 members. So women were joining and involved in many movements and associations in Stirling. They craved their independence, equality and wanted their voices to be heard.

Lavinia Malcolm (provost from Dollar) and **Annie Barlow** (councillor from Callander) both supported women's suffrage. They were the only two women to attend the Convention of Royal Burghs in 1914. Previously a draft report incorporated the inclusion of women's votes into the Scottish Home Rule Bill. However, the Annual Committee had removed this, so the ladies asked for its re-insertion. In parliament, the Bill was thrown out after a second reading after much debating about the women's enfranchisement clause.

Chrystal Macmillan in 1915 (fifth from right). (Courtesy of LSE Library)

Ethel Moorhead (Johnson) was probably one of the well-known suffragettes when she visited Stirling. Her defiance was evident in 1912 when she attempted to smash the glass case surrounding the Wallace Sword.

Although this feisty suffragette was born in Kent in 1869, and trained as an artist abroad, when her parents moved to Dundee in 1900, she eventually returned to look after them. She was well-known among the suffragettes as the first woman in Scotland to be force-fed in prison in 1914.

Ethel was arrested several times and imprisoned. She once threw an egg at Winston Churchill, was charged with several arson attacks, threw pepper at police and wrecked some of the police cells. Not a woman to mess with.

As mentioned on pages 39/40, **Rhoda Robinson (Craig)** arrived in Dunblane by train with another suffragette and was followed by police. She was accused of starting a fire in Stirlingshire, but some time later charges were dropped.

There were undoubtedly many more suffragettes in Stirling and the surrounding areas, but a larger publication would be necessary to record them all.

There were many men who supported the cause for women, too. One such man was Reverend Robert Primrose. In 1914, he spoke at a WSPU meeting claiming that many who did not support the women's vote showed contempt for a person's rights. Many husbands and male relatives supported the females in their fight to vote. There was the Men's Political Union for Women's Enfranchisement (MPU) (formed in 1910 by Victor Duval), the Men's League for Women's Suffrage (MLWS) (1907), and the Northern Men's Federation (NMF) (1913).

It is believed that the suffrage campaigners in Stirling, male and female, were in the main, middle-class people.

Sir Henry Campbell-Bannerman, educated in Glasgow, became Liberal prime minister in 1906, with Stirling as his constituency. In theory, he supported the suffrage movement, telling the women to 'keep pestering, and exercise the virtue of patience'. This angered many women, though, who had already been doing so for some time.

The term suffragette rather than suffragist came about around this period. A *Daily Mail* reporter, Charles Hands, dubbed the militant women suffragettes, following their revolts.

Many of these middle-class women were also found working in temperance, and other social groups that were concerned with the plights of working-class women. Fighting for the suffrage cause they probably felt helped less fortunate women who were often overworked, underpaid and exploited. The right to women's votes would help those working women's positions, or so the suffragettes and suffragists thought.

A WSPU meeting in Stirling in 1908 saw a **Miss G. Conolan** from Glasgow, stating just this observation. Both her grandfathers had been MPs, and this woman was heavily involved in suffrage.

In 1908, Campbell-Bannerman died and Liberal Herbert Asquith took over the reins as prime minister. He was opposed greatly to women's votes. There was much bell-ringing, sandwich-board advertising and public speaking in Stirling town by the suffragettes.

W.H. Lamond was a suffragette from the Edinburgh society who wanted speakers for the islands. She came to Stirling in autumn 1909 and spoke about women's long work hours and the type of employment, stating that unless their voices were heard, the problems could not be solved.

So many women were passionate about their cause and, more often than not, concerned about the welfare of these less fortunate women.

Between 1908 and 1912, although there was no formation of a Stirling branch of WSPU, many meetings were held on the campaign trail. With the Conciliation Bills of 1910, 1911 and 1912 put forward, favouring just over a million women who owned property, this went back and forth in parliament, but nothing concrete came of it. The 1912 Manhood Franchise Bill also never came to much.

From 1912, incidents occurred with the suffragettes. As mentioned above Ethel Moorhead (Johnson) smashed the Wallace Sword glass case, leaving a note documented by the local paper, the *Stirling Observer,* saying:

> Your liberties were won by the sword. Release the women who are fighting for their liberties. Stop the forcible feeding in Dublin.

The words speak for themselves.

Maude Allan, Violet Asquith, Catherine Douglas and **Margo Tennant** (all false names) were suffragettes who attacked Prime Minister Herbert Asquith in Bannockburn, just outside Stirling, with red pepper and attempted to hit him with a dog whip. They were arrested and bailed for £10 each and then released without charge.

Even Aithrey Spa Bowling Green, in nearby Bridge of Allan, suffered under militant females as deep incisions were made into the green with words 'Justice for women before bowls'. Sometimes the suffragettes' passion may have been so strong it outweighed their judgement and morals when attacking prominent people and causing destruction.

There were many, of course, against the women's enfranchisement that included women as well as men. Some felt that women in direct competition with the men would harm the women's positions.

The Scottish Anti-Suffrage League was formed in Scotland by the **Duchess of Montrose,** but it appears there were only fourteen societies throughout Scotland. There were branches in nearby Dollar and Kirkcaldy.

In 1913, in Stirling, there was talk of a branch being set up there, and a Mrs Fraser would have been secretary. But there appears to be no further mention of this in the local papers.

CHAPTER SIX

Highlands and Islands

Brief history

As this is a large area of Scotland to cover, this section will focus on the large cities and towns of these Highlands and Islands.

Scotland has a total of approximately 790 islands off the Scottish coastline. However, not all are inhabited. According to the 2011 census, there are ninety-three islands with inhabitants. A total of 103,702 people lived on Scottish islands in March 2011.

A table of islands with more than 2,000 inhabitants (figures from NRS)

Lewis & Harris	21,031 (largest island)
Mainland Shetland	18,765
Mainland Orkney	17,162
Skye	10,008
Bute	6,498
Islay	3,228
Mull	2,800
Arran	4,629

According to the census, the male population for the islands is slightly higher than the female population. No figure was given. Seventeen islands have five or fewer people living on them, according to the census.

Some of the islands have bridges connecting them to the mainland, such as Skye. Others are connected to the larger islands by a bridge, such as Orkney connects to four smaller islands and so does Shetland. A causeway connects a few other tiny islands to larger ones. The Gaelic word for island is *Eilean*. The Gaelic language is still spoken in many of the islands today.

Some of the islands have many things to offer, such as Shetland with its ponies, Arran with its beautiful scenery and Harris (and Lewis) with Harris Tweed. Some of the larger islands have their own whisky distilleries, such as Mull, Arran, Skye and Orkney.

The Highlands are classed as the area on the Great Glen, which is 62 miles long and runs from west Scotland and Fort William through to Inverness on the edge of the Moray Firth. This includes approximately 50 miles of land to the east of the Great Glen.

Most people consider that Inverness is the capital of the Highlands. As with the islands, up in the Highlands there are many distilleries, such as Oban, Ben Nevis, Aberfeldy, etc. The mountains in the Highlands include Ben Nevis, the highest in the British Isles

Historically, with the 1745 Jacobite Rising, a great number of Highlanders emigrated to America. The Highland Clearances in the eighteenth and nineteenth centuries, saw aristocratic land owners evict their tenant farmers and replace them with grazing sheep. Therefore, many Highlanders emigrated to the coast or to the Lowlands, urban areas, and abroad. Some tenants did not want to go and there was a good deal of violence around this time.

With the tenant farmers gone, landowners could charge higher rents for sheep farmers. It also meant they had fewer tenants to worry about and collect rent from, and there was less administration.

Crofting became popular in the west Highlands and Islands in the nineteenth century, and it appears from photographs that women often fertilised the ground by hand with seaweed.

Population by area in the Highlands 2013 (figures from Highland Council from NRS)

Badenoch & Strathspey	13,561
Caithness	26,067
Inverness	79,415
Lochaber	19,943
Nairn	12,945
Ross & Cromarty	54,124
Skye & Lochalsh	13,045
Sutherland	13,841

In 2012, it was estimated by the Highland Council that there are approximately 4,500 more females than men.

Working life

Crofting was a way of life for many Highlanders and Islanders in the nineteenth century. Women milked the cows, made butter and cheese, and stockings were often knitted from the wool they spun from their own sheep. Gairloch was particularly well known for its hand-made stockings. In Harris and Shetland, as in many of the islands, there was plenty of knitting, and the women used their own spun wool.

The work for crofter women (and men) was often hard and the elements did not help. Children usually engaged in clearing stones and boulders from the land in order to sow crops of barley, oats and potatoes.

Crofting came about as a result of Highland Clearances, but quite often the food they produced was on a small scale and had to be supplemented with fishing, spinning, weaving and kelp-making. It was the men who fished and the women who spun commercially in Orkney, and they made money from spinning lint.

In Bute, Argyll, Kintyre, western and highland Perthshire and the east of Scotland, the female workforce dealt with linen. A great number of women protested on the islands when the Clearances took place. In 1882, there was the Battle of the Braes on Skye. Because some of the men were working away from home, or serving in the military, the women fought to save the land they had worked on.

According to Lyn Abrams' book on Shetland, Highlander men were often seen as the main crofters. But on Shetland it was the women who were at the forefront on the farmland.

A minister from south-west Scotland in 1861 commented: 'Most of the work on Shetland is done by women. They do the indoor work as well as the outdoor work.'

In Shetland, some of the men went to sea, fishing or whaling, so the women were left to cut peats, tend to livestock, carry manure to the fields, and dig and plant out their ground, as well as run a household and deal with any children they may have had. A very hard and gruelling life.

In the 1900s, fishing, mainly herring, was a thriving business and women were used in more than 123 curing stations from Unst to Grutness. The women came from the Highlands and Islands to seek employment, which usually lasted twelve to sixteen weeks. They worked in threes, consisting of two gutters and one packer, and they lived in small huts nearby. This employment helped nearly 4,000 females bring money into their families. The women and girls worked long hours, usually from 6am until 6pm for a wage of approximately £10-£12 per season. It seems the girls had a camaraderie, despite the hardships.

The 1930s saw a decline in the herring, and work for women was no longer available.

Even then they fought for their rights. A strike came about while they were working at Yarmouth. They wanted a pay rise, and after a week of striking their determination won. They received a shilling per barrel (a rise of 2 pence).

In a recent article by Theresa Mackay, she revealed that she had found documents on innkeepers in the nineteenth century in the Highlands and Islands, and a majority appear to have been women. They had to deal with drovers, businessmen and people with money on holiday. They appeared to be tough women, but many kept the business running smoothly and peacefully (in the main).

Industrialisation in most parts of Scotland made an impression on the workforce. However, in the Highlands and Islands in 1911, agriculture was still seen as the main source of work in the area, with forty-one per cent of the population engaged here.

In the First World War, females were employed by the Queen Mary's Needlework Guild to knit and sew garments for soldiers and sailors. Many Shetland women were involved in this venture. Lerwick, on Shetland, had a naval base where the Women's Royal Naval Service (WRNS) (formed in 1917) helped serve their country. They were initially employed with mundane jobs such as cleaning, but soon became useful as telephone operators during the war. Girl guides (along with boy scouts) were often used to deliver messages to this naval base during this war.

Health & welfare

There was a distinct lack of doctors in some of these remote places. In Inverness, uncertified deaths amounted to approximately forty-two per cent. Because men and women were spread over a greater area in these rural surroundings, the death rate was lower than in the cities in the 1800s. The fact they were breathing in fresh air rather than smog may have helped.

However, towards the end of that century, TB was rife. Workers returning from the Lowlands brought the condition with them. Most crofters lived in basic buildings such as the blackhouses of the nineteenth century and, although the roof was of a wooden frame, turf, heather and thatch were used to make the walls and roofs of houses. The floor was usually mud, and very often, because there were no chimneys or windows in buildings, the smoke lingered. Typhoid and cholera were other persistent diseases that stayed longer in these areas.

In 1845, the Poor Law (Scotland) Act saw the responsibility of medical aid to the poor change from the church to the state. A medical officer was appointed by the Poor Law Medical Services to attend patients in remote areas.

Women doctors assigned to the crofting communities, it seems, had to prove they were willing to work in the harsh conditions of these regions, despite the fact many male doctors would not attend.

Reaching some of the remote areas involved hard, arduous journeys for some of the medical profession to attend their patients. Even in the twentieth century, travelling by car wasn't always easy due to poor roads. Nurses attending the sick often travelled by bicycle or motorbike, and then on foot.

To summon medical practitioners in the nineteenth and early twentieth centuries, the Highlands and Islands required telephones or the telegraph, which to begin with was limited.

The Napier Report in the late 1800s commented on the insanitary conditions of the remote areas, their housing (which sometimes cattle shared), finances, etc. The poorest conditions were found on Lewis and Shetland. Water supplies for residents in these areas was often poor, with women drawing water from wells or streams, which were often contaminated. This in turn caused diseases such as typhus and enteric fever.

The potato famine in the mid-1800s was obviously not beneficial to the crofters and farmers. More food was imported and sometimes their diets suffered. A Medical Research Council's report in the 1940s found that, due to sugary, starchy diets, a great deal of Highlanders' dental health had deteriorated.

In 1900, there were thirty-two trained Queen's jubilee nurses in the Highlands and Islands, and forty-nine in 1912. These, of course, did not work in every area. There were also less trained govan nurses, who dealt with midwifery issues and were sent to decrease the dependence of local, untrained women who had previously helped to deliver babies in their remote areas. Only twenty-nine hospitals were noted in the Highlands and Islands in 1912, and most of these were twenty-bedded and under. Inverness was the largest with sixty-eight beds.

In 1913, the Highlands & Islands Medical Service (HIMS) was created. Although this was not a free service, the fees were of a minimal amount, enabling many people to receive treatment. In 1948, the NHS took over this service.

Although this has nothing to do with suffrage directly, indirectly it helps to understand the background of many Scottish women and the hardships, inequality and suchlike that they have endured throughout history. Because of this in the periods prior to women's enfranchisement, proud Scottish women fought to gain leadership, equality and not be regarded by some as 'second-rate citizens'. That is, of course, not to say that men have not had hardships through history as well, but as this book focuses on women, consequently the menfolk are only mentioned where relevant.

Education

In the mid-1800s, only half of Highland dwellers could write, and about one-sixth could not read. Figures for women able to write their own names in Scotland in general was lower than men in the nineteenth century, but lower still in the Highlands and Islands. In these areas, Gaelic and English were spoken. But studies show that the former was not always known by some teachers employed and thus proved problematic.

In the north and west Highlands, the Gaelic language was more prevalent. The schools were widely dispersed and so were the attendees, who often had to work the land to support the family. This was the same situation as poorer city children who, in the nineteenth and twentieth centuries often worked and, therefore, attended school less regularly than they should have.

Several organisations were in place to help with the teaching of Highlanders and Islanders, such as the Scotland Society for Propagating Christian Knowledge (SSPCK) and the Assembly of the Church of Scotland Schools. However, in a statistical account by J. Sinclair, when the SSPCK commenced in the early eighteenth century, one school only had six girls compared to thirty-nine boys. It would seem work for the girls was uppermost, although this did improve slightly for girls in the mid-1800s.

In 1864, the Argyll Commission was established to investigate schooling in Lowlands and the Highlands. Assistant commissioner Alexander Nicholson reported that the Isle of Skye had very poor literacy for girls over the age of 16. He went on to say that job opportunities for women were poor unless they were going into domestic service or seasonal work in the fields and on the shores. According to him, on the Isle of Lewis, although women could speak Gaelic, only a small proportion spoke English, and in the latter part of the 1800s on Lewis, only 684 girls attended school compared to 922 boys. A total of 423 girls did not even attend school. It was felt learning was not as important for a girl as it was a boy.

The 1872 Education (Scotland) Act did make primary schooling mandatory, but also prohibited speaking Gaelic. Nicholson reported that improvement for females was noted although not perfect. In 1900, in Inverness, at Duisdale Public School, it was noted by a teacher that absentee boys were busy at home working seaweed. Non-attendance by girls was not noted at all.

To help with the financial situation in the Highlands, a subsidy known as the Highland Minute was established in 1885. This help ceased in 1908, but three schools in Lewis were apparently still receiving this funding. History proves the inequality for girls and women, as they were seen as home-makers and it wasn't (in most cases) necessary to give them a good education as they probably didn't or wouldn't use it.

Suffrage, politics, women and notable men

Flora Drummond (the General) (1878-1949). Although born in Manchester, Flora Drummond spent her childhood living with her parents on the Isle of Arran. As a teenager she trained in Glasgow for a business qualification to enable her to work as a postmistress. However, this did not come to fruition, as she was an inch (2.5cm) under the required height.

She married Joseph Drummond at the age of 20 and moved back to Manchester where she worked in a factory making baby linen, although some sources say she worked at the Oliver typewriter company. The couple were both involved with the Independent Labour Party and the Fabian Society (British Socialist Organisation). It seems Flora was outraged about the low wages of women, and lack of employment for them at the time, and this may have encouraged her into suffrage.

Flora possibly joined the WSPU in 1905, but it was in 1906 that she appears to have become fully involved. She was arrested several times in London due to protesting around Downing Street. She was imprisoned in Holloway in 1908, but was released as she was pregnant. She even named her child Keir Hardie Drummond, after Keir Hardie, the Scottish politician and Labour leader who strongly supported women's suffrage.

In October 1909, she proudly led a march in Edinburgh astride a horse. She wore a military style uniform (hence the General title).

A meeting held at St Andrews Hall, Glasgow, in March 1914 saw Flora take to the platform and speak militantly. Mrs Pankhurst had been due to speak at the meeting but had been arrested. Flora went on to talk at Edinburgh and Dundee.

Flora Drummond (centre). (Courtesy of LSE Library)

The fiery suffragette was reported to have been arrested in May 1914 and then she returned to Arran to recover from her ordeal of a hunger strike in prison. She went back to London a few months later, at the start of the First World War.

Afterwards, she co-founded the Women's Guild of Empire, but this organisation stirred up vitriolic comments from her former militant partner, Nora Elam (a militant suffragette born in Ireland but living in London).

Flora eventually went back to Scotland after her second husband died in 1944, and she lived in Carradale, which overlooks the Isle of Arran; her childhood home. She died from a stroke in 1949.

It wasn't until 2001 that a gravestone in Brackley Cemetery, Carradale, was erected for Flora – The Suffragette General. Until then she sadly had an unmarked grave.

Christina Jamieson (1870-1942) was born on Shetland, at Sandness. Her father was a teacher on the island. Her brothers were given a good education, whereas she was taught home-making. She did write non-fiction and fiction about Shetland for several publications, sometimes under the name of John Cranston. In 1909, she published a brief history of suffrage entitled *Sketch of votes for women movement*.

She became secretary of the Shetland Suffrage Society, which was connected to the NUWSS.

At the coronation of King George V in 1911, she represented Shetland in a March of England's Women in honour of the event. She also designed the banner that was used.

She always believed, according to the *Biographical Dictionary of Scottish Women*, that women should be given the vote due to their

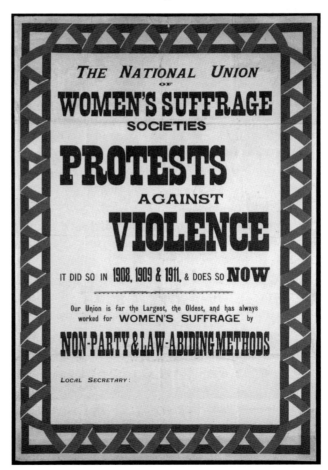

NUWSS poster.
(Courtesy of
LSE Library)

constant industry and self-independence, their patient, unselfish and faithful rearing of men. Living on Shetland, she often saw the hardships of women working the land.

According to Esther Breitenbach's book on Scottish women, Christina believed that of 4,000 votes on Shetland, many of the seamen were away and could not use their vote. She felt enfranchisement of women would possibly help with pressure on future legislation enabling better working conditions and wages for their seamen, and not just a vote for women. They would be contributing to the economy of Shetland.

The Shetland Society was often not happy that the island was often ignored by prominent speakers, as many visited north Scotland but not always the Isles. Politician Ethel Snowden (ILP) was invited to Shetland by Christina in a bid to influence the island women of the reasoning behind enfranchisement of women.

In 1916, Christina lived in Lerwick on Shetland and is believed to be the first female to take up a post with a public organisation, the Lerwick School Board.

Christina died in New Zealand in 1942, after emigrating seven years prior to her death in an endeavour to alleviate some of her asthma symptoms.

Jessie Saxby (1842-1940) was born in Unst, one of the Shetland Islands. With a doctor for a father and her mother a writer, Jessie became the author of forty-seven books, and a suffragette. Her books and various articles were often about Shetland.

She married at the age of 17 and moved to Inveraray, where she bore six children, one of whom died. Then she lived in Edinburgh for a time after the death of her husband in 1873.

In 1890, she returned to her roots in Unst and became a member of the Shetland Suffrage Society, possibly using her writing skills for the suffrage campaign. Jessie was a member of the Temperance Society, which several suffragettes over the years were.

While on Unst, she lived at Wullver's Hool which, in 2016, came up for sale with offers over £25,000.

Harriet Leisk (1853-1951) was chairman of the Shetland Women's Suffrage Society (SWSS), but in the First World War she headed the Emergency Helpers in Shetland with a band of seventeen committee members and fifty other women helping. The aim of the group was to help with the war effort by collecting unwanted clothing to give to poorly servicemen and women who may have been injured locally, first aid lessons and handing out food and essentials such as bedding and hot water bottles.

Some SWSS members tended servicemen's graves that had been left in disrepair.

Much of the work of the society in Shetland and other islands pre-war was often non-militant, but with a view to using propaganda and pamphlets to highlight all women's plight for the enfranchisement. The Highlands and Islands, as with other areas in Scotland during the First World War, ceased the suffrage cause and dedicated its resources and woman-power to helping the war effort.

Marion Wallace Dunlop (1864-1942) was born in Inverness, at Leys Castle. However, she spent most of her life in London. Her other connection to Scotland, apart from family now in Kippen, was she claimed she was named after Scotsman William Wallace's alleged wife Marion Braidfute.

She joined the London WSPU, but was also an illustrator with two children's books to her credit. Marion exhibited her illustrations around the country, including Scotland.

She appears to have been the first woman, in 1909, in Britain to go on hunger strike in prison. She had been arrested for damaging property in the House of Commons with a rubber stamp. She was released after ninety-one hours. There does not appear to be any mention of whether she spoke in Scotland for the suffrage cause.

The Highlands and Islands did not have as many high-profile women born to the area as maybe the major cities and towns, but all the local women who fought for the vote did so with gusto, which is evident from scanning the WEA (Workers Education Association) suffrage timeline data.

Prominent speakers visited the Highlands and Islands to rally women to enfranchisement. Here are a few names and dates:

1871	**Jane Taylour** and **Agnes McLaren** visited Inverness, Tain, Forres, Elgin, Wick, Invergordon, Dingwall. Societies were likely formed in 1872/74 in Dingwall, Thurso, Wick and Tain.
1873	**Jessie Craigen** spoke at Forres, Nairn, Auldearn, Grantown, Fortrose and Rosemarkie.
1907/09/10	**Helen Fraser** visited Inverness, Caithness, Dingwall and Nairn.
1909	**Adela Pankhurst** attended meeting at Inverness in May.
1909	**Wilhemina Hay Abbot** from the Edinburgh NUWSS spoke at Inverness in June.
1909/10/11	**Emmeline** and **Adela Pankhurst** spoke at Grantown on Spey, Fort William, Tain, Inverness, Invergordon, Aviemore, Dingwall and Nairn at various times during these years.
1909	**Chrystal Macmillan** visited Orkney, Helmsdale, Brora, Dornoch, Cromarty, Golspie, and Alness.
1909/11	**Lady Frances Balfour** spoke at meetings in Nairn and Inverness in October 1909 and at Oban in October 1911.
1910	**Millicent Garret Fawcett** visited in September as her sister owned a home there.
1912	**Dr Elsie Inglis** visits Shetland, Orkney, Wick, Tain, John O'Groats and Dingwall. She was honorary secretary of the Scottish Federation of Women's Suffrage Societies. Anti-suffrage meetings were held all over Scotland, but in Nairn for instance, in November 1909, one was held by the Countess of Leven and Melville along with a Mrs Arthur Somervell from London. At the meeting the presiding gentleman, Mr A. Mackintosh, said: 'The natural sphere for a woman was not the political arena with all its muddy waters, but her own home, and to attend to her domestic duties, and do good to all around her.'

This was often the thought process of a great deal of men (and some women) in those authoritarian times.

VOTES FOR WOMEN.

Miss ADELA PANKHURST,

*Organiser, National Women's
Social and Political Union,
4, Clement's Inn, Strand, W.C.*

Right: Adela Pankhurst.
(Courtesy of LSE Library)

Below left: Chrystal
Macmillan spoke in
Orkney and Shetland.
(Courtesy of LSE Library)

Below right: Emmeline
Pankhurst (in black) in
Elgin 1907. (Courtesy of
LSE Library)

Mr J. Malcolm Mitchell, honorary political secretary for the Men's League for Women's Suffrage, held meetings in and around Inverness in 1912 in a bid to help women's enfranchisement.

Cathcart Wasson (1848-1921) was a Liberal Unionist MP for Orkney and Shetland from 1900 until his death in April 1921. Originally born in Ayrshire, he lived in New Zealand then moved back to Scotland when he took up the position for Orkney and Shetland. Despite many votes in favour of the Conciliation Bills 1910/11/12, which would extend the right to vote for over a million women, Cathcart, along with many other MPs, was against any female enfranchisement. It is believed the MPs felt that if women got the vote they would choose another political party rather than theirs.

The Shetland Women's Suffrage Society did in fact write to the Liberal chairman asking that Cathcart Wasson, their MP, discard his opposition to the Conciliation Bill of 1911. It seems he did not.

Lilias Mitchell (Scottish) and **Elsie Howie** (English) were notable in the Highlands for a suffragette attack (see page 77). There appears to be very little militant (documented) action taken in the Highlands and Islands.

Herbert Asquith in London but attacked in Dornoch. (Courtesy of LSE Library)

Another incident reported in the *Highland Times* in 1914 was a fire at Hazelbank House, Tomatin. It was unclear if it was the suffragettes, as the *Highland Times* quotes no suffrage literature was left in the vicinity. But the *New York Times*, who also published a piece on the fire, quoted there was. Very often this was the suffragettes' calling card.

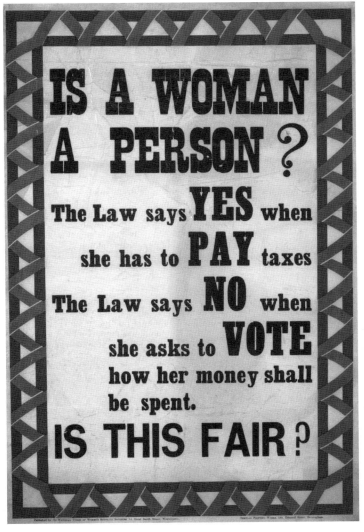

'Is a woman a person' poster. (Courtesy of LSE Library)

CHAPTER SEVEN

Dumfries and Galloway

Brief history

This area covers most of the south-west of Scotland. Originally three counties, Dumfrieshire, Kirkcudbrightshire and Wigtownshire, became known as Dumfries and Galloway in about 1975 when there was a local government reorganisation.

Robert Burns the Scottish poet, Gretna Green, Lockerbie (plane disaster of 1988), James Matthew Barrie (*Peter Pan* author who spent his childhood in Dumfries), and Moffatt (Woollen Mill) are all associated with Dumfries and Galloway. Burns' cottage was connected to the suffragettes.

Doonhammers is the name sometimes given to the people of Dumfries, the market town of the area which is situated on the east bank of the River Nith that flows into the Solway Firth. Dumfries is also known as the Queen of the South, a name given to the area by local poet David Dunbar. The name Dumfries originates from the word dun, or *dun phreas*, meaning the fort, or brushwood ridge. The tweed making industry was popular in Dumfries, until the twentieth century when it ceased, and then products such as knitwear, hosiery, rubber and canned milk took over.

Galloway comes from the Gaelic *Gallgaidhel* meaning land of the stranger. Inhabitants of Galloway are known as Gallovidians or Galwegians. Galloway was well-known for its horses, which sadly were cross-bred and appear to now be extinct. Galloway cattle have been established since the seventeenth century (for milk and beef).

It is reported the oldest person in Scotland lived in Trigony Country House (now a hotel, once used as a lodge for nearby Closeburn Castle), north of Dumfries. She was Mrs Frances

Shackerly, who lived at the house and died here aged 107, although some reports say 109.

Stranraer to the west of Dumfries was, until 2011, a ferry port for travellers to Northern Ireland.

Population

1861	Males = 76,437	Females = 87,174
1911	Males = 68,267	Females = 75,129
1951	Males = 72,362	Females = 76,100
1981	Males = 68,051	Females = 71,811
2001	Males = 71,300	Females = 76,460
2011	Males = 73,405	Females = 77,919
2015	Males = 72,691	Females = 76,979

Working life

Linen and textiles, as with previous areas mentioned, were large employers of women and girls in the early and mid-1800s. A total of 45 acres was devoted to flax in Lower Annandale. The women and girls used spinning wheels at home to spin the flax, which was then passed on to weavers who made it into cloths.

Sanquhar was the eighteenth-century centre for hand-knitting. Garments, especially gloves, were knitted in two tone colours by the women of the area in a bid to earn a living.

According to the Future Museum, in the 1920s, local woman Jessie Wilson knitted socks and gloves for a living. With intricate patterns and fine needles and yarns, these hand-knitted garments were a treasure to behold. Jessie received a personal thank-you letter in 1935 from Lady Alice Scott for her present of Sanquhar gloves to her ladyship and her husband the Duke of Gloucester.

Nearby Crawick Mill brought more employment, with a new carpet factory.

From the late 1800s, hosiery factories sprung up in Dumfries – five in total – bringing more employment to the area. James McGeorge was the largest hosiery factory, which employed many young women to manufacture the garments.

Family farms often benefited from a farmer's wife, especially regarding the cows – milking and all the by-products that entailed, such as cheese and butter. It has been said that farms in Dumfries often employed men for the land as long as the wives tended to the milking. It was, however, a very long day. Dairying meant rising as early as 5am to milk for possibly a couple of hours, back to the house to work on domestic duties, make lunch, feed the cows, make tea, and then milking again, before finally collapsing in bed. Agricultural work for women was often seasonal, hence the reason for knitting, wool-spinning and straw-plaiting. Often children were sent into service to bring in the money in order to survive.

In 1911, agriculture in Dumfries and Galloway was the largest employer (just second behind the Highlands). Industrialisation had made its impact on other areas of Scotland, but there was no such outcome here.

In the late 1800s, the Lowlands did see many female rural workers ditch their hard agricultural employment and seek domestic work in cities. A royal commission stated:

> It was the obligation of employers in rural areas to provide better cottages and higher wages to compete with enticement of town life.

Jumping ahead to 1915, a government munitions factory was built just outside Gretna, which had two townships and four production factories and is believed to have been the largest cordite (low explosive) factory in the UK, some say in the world, at the time. More than 11,500 women worked there in 1917 compared to approximately 5,000 men. The townships had their own bakery, medical office, police force and laundry facilities.

Another company, The North British Rubber Company, produced 1,185,000 pairs of boots for the army in the First World War. They again supplied boots for the Second World War as well as groundsheets, gas masks and lifebelts. After the Second World War, the company needed larger premises and moved to Heathall in Dumfries. Many women worked in the factories and were paid by the piece. According to *NBR Wrinklies*, a website for retired workers of the company, employee women (and men) seemed to have been looked after reasonably well, with a warm dining hall and clean working conditions for all. However, discrepancy in pay reared its head, with women paid 10-14 shillings (10 shillings is around £18 in today's money) for a fifty-seven-hour week, while the men were paid higher wages.

In 1920, Dorothee Pullinger became manager of the Galloway Motor Company (her father T.C. Pullinger managed the Arrol-Johnston site in Kirkcudbright). This resilient female employed many local women in her factory, which bore the colours of the suffragettes. An apprentice course was set up for the women, which ran for three years only, compared to one for the men, who trained for five years. It was believed by the company that the women learnt faster.

Dorothee also helped manage and design production with her father on the Galloway car, built in 1924. The car was aimed at women, due to the fact it was lighter and smaller.

Even today only nine per cent of women in the UK are engineers, so what Dorothee managed to achieve in Galloway was a major feat for women.

Health & welfare

Cholera struck in Dumfries and Galloway in 1832 and 1848, with deaths totalling nearly 1,000. Sanitation was poor and overcrowding led to the virulent spread of TB, not just in the Lowlands, but also with migrant workers in Dumfries, who then returned to their homes in the Highlands taking the disease with them.

The Annan Combination Hospital was built as an infectious diseases hospital in 1895 and was probably used to house TB patients. In Scotland, TB was a big killer of people both in the Highlands and in the Lowlands.

Kirkcudbright Poorhouse was built in 1849, but by 1946 it was deemed as unfit for the sick and aged. In 1853, an almshouse, called

Kirkpatrick Fleming, was built for the poor. It housed twenty-seven residents according to the 1881 census, eleven of whom were female and, of those female inhabitants, three were under 5 years of age. The women's section housed the kitchen, laundry, scullery and ironing room. The men just had a store room, a sick room and a day room.

Crichton Royal Hospital was founded in 1828 with fifty private patients and fifty pauper patients, and was originally a lunatic asylum. It has been suggested by some historians that some people were incarcerated in these institutions for just being inconvenient.

Throughout Scotland there were very few school dentists and by the mid-1930s, there was only one dentist per 11,000 children. This was surprisingly low given that a tenth of their diet at the time was jam and sugar.

Education

Until the end of the nineteenth century, girls from working-class backgrounds who could attend school invariably didn't. Cooking and sewing were normal activities for the girls in Dumfries, but sadly poverty within their families prevented them from attending. Quite simply the parents could not afford the materials needed for sewing and cooking.

A Mrs Black from Glasgow in the late 1800s did write to the Dumfries burgh school board stating she was going to commence evening cookery classes for girls, and the school board supported her in this decision. She had the help of three female teachers, paid for by the board, and gave discounted fees for older girls attending the sessions. In Laurieston village, three girls were even given free attendance to the cookery classes, as they were above the standard required.

The 1872 Education Act helped to improve literacy all over Scotland and by the early 1900s, illiteracy was almost eliminated and improvement seen in school attendance.

Andrew Carnegie, who was born in Dunfermline, Fife, set up the Carnegie Trust for Universities in Scotland in 1901 which assisted students at university. Although helpful in these times for women, in the late nineteenth and early twentieth centuries, women were often excluded from higher education.

Widow Elizabeth Crichton of Dumfries in the mid-1800s was believed to have wanted a university in the town, but this was rejected and her money was used to fund a lunatic asylum instead. However, in 1899 plans were for male and female admission and infirmary units. These were completed in 1904.

In 1916, the Dumfries school board added war cookery to the children's curriculum. It is not known whether this was for both sexes, but it was more likely for the females.

According to Richard Finlay's *Modern Scotland*, in 1938, female teachers were paid £20 per year less than their male counterparts. A majority of male teachers tended to have degrees, approximately seven out of ten, whereas only three out of ten women had them. Only unmarried women could become full-time teachers in this period and earlier. However, private schools may have taken on some married women.

It seems whether you were a young female at school in the nineteenth and twentieth centuries, or a female teacher in Scotland (and England), times for most were hard, with discrimination against female teachers, quite often many domestic lessons for the young girls, but very little academic tuition, as they were generally only thought of as home-makers.

Women, suffrage, politics and notable men

Jane E. Taylour (1827-1905) was born in Inch, Stranraer. From her early forties, Jane visited many areas throughout Scotland to talk about suffrage and equality in education and employment. Her talk in Edinburgh in 1873 was well reported in the *Scotsman*. In her speech, Jane said that most people opposed to votes for women felt a woman's place was in the home and they should not be entered into anything in public life. Jane went on to say that this was strange in a country governed by a queen.

Between 1870 and 1872, she was honorary secretary of the NSWS for Galloway and joint secretary with Agnes McLaren of the

Edinburgh Society. Jane and Agnes visited many areas, including remote places such as Orkney and Shetland. Leaving Scotland for England in the late 1800s, she became secretary of the British Temperance Society.

Doctor Flora Murray (1869-1923) was born in Dumfries. She commenced her medical career in the London School of Medicine and completed her training in Durham in 1903. It appears she worked for a couple of years in Scotland before heading down to London in 1905.

She was a member of the WSPU in 1908 and, along with her friend Doctor Louisa Garret Anderson (who was English but schooled in St Andrews, Fife), set up a nursing home for injured suffragettes in Notting Hill.

Both these suffragette lady doctors founded the Women's Hospital for Children in London, with the suffragette motto of Deeds Not Words.

Flora Murray. (Courtesy of LSE Library)

In 1916, they again ran a 573-bedded military hospital in Endell Street, Covent Garden, London. One of their achievements, apart from caring for the sick and injured, was that both these hospitals were staffed mainly with women, both medical and non-medical. The suffragette motto was used again.

A plaque commemorating the two doctors is now on the site of the hospital, which ceased in 1919.

Lady Florence Dixie (1855-1905) was born in Cummitrees, Dumfries. Her father died in a possible shooting accident, so she and her siblings were whisked off to Paris.

Florence married at the age of 19 and went to live in Leicester. However, she was to return to Kinmount in Scotland in the 1880s. She was a lover of writing and wrote for the *Morning Post* and penned several books. In 1890, one book, *Gloriana, or The Revolution of 1900*, appeared to be ahead of its time. The story has women getting the vote and at the end it jumps to 1999 and women are governing Britain. All of this was written in 1890. Did she have foresight? Or was it hope?

Some say she was a member of the NUWSS. She most definitely believed in equality for women. Florence was a keen supporter of suffrage and rational dress movements and it was because of the latter that she endorsed the British Ladies Football Team.

In a letter in 1895 to the *Pall Mall Gazette,* she wrote:

> Let women go in for this most excellent game and earn for themselves that improved physique, which will not only improve their appearance but health as well. It may act as an incentive to the rising generation to do likewise.

Her association with the club meant a great deal of press coverage was given to the matches.

Although ladies have played football since as early as 1628, according to church records in Lanarkshire, it was only in 1998 that Scotland's lady footballers were governed by the Scottish Football Association (SFA).

Lady Florence Dixie sent in
by Stuart Gibbs.

Historian Stuart Gibbs, who has researched Lady Flo, said:

> A lot is made of gender politics, but class and position were also
> important factors.' Has that changed a great deal in today's current
> climate?

Vera (Jack) Holme (1881-1969). Although born in Lancashire,
Vera lived a great deal of her life in Kirkcudbright from 1919.
However, before the war she was well-known as the Pankhurst's
chauffeur, and she dressed accordingly. A suffragette and an actress,
she joined the Women's Volunteer Reserve in the war and then went
onto join the Scottish Women's Hospitals for Foreign Service,
which Scottish suffragette Doctor Elsie Inglis was involved with.

In 1911, Vera was involved romantically with suffragette
Eveline Haverfield (originally from Kingussie). She died in 1969 in
a Glasgow Nursing Home.

Right: Vera Holme in uniform. (Courtesy of LSE Library)

Below: Vera Holme as chauffeur. (Courtesy of LSE Library)

Christian Jane Fergusson (1876-1957) was born in Maxwelltown, Dumfries. She was a Scottish painter. She was schooled at Dumfries Academy and trained at Crystal Palace School of Art, London.

Chris (or Chrissy) as she was known, was a student and then tutor at Glasgow School of Art. She also taught art at Kirkcudbright Academy.

As with most female artists of her generation, Chris probably felt it was a struggle to be accepted on equal terms as male artists. Her grandson, Jim Henderson, wrote a piece in the *Scottish Review* 2011 stating she was 'an active and passionate suffragette', and he felt she had embraced suffrage possibly because of her profession as an artist and wanting to be taken seriously.

As a member of the Glasgow Society of Lady Artists Club, Chris won the Lauder Prize in 1922, 1938 and 1954, for best oil painting in show.

John William Gulland (1864-1920) was a Liberal MP for Dumfries in 1906. He backed the women in their cause for enfranchisement. According to author Chris Wrigley, three-quarters of Scottish Liberal MPs supported votes for women.

In 1907, the Scottish and English Women's Liberal Federation spoke to MPs who were sympathetic to their cause. A request for a ballot at the next parliament session was put forward. A Bill was proposed to give some women and all men the vote. It never came to fruition as it was dropped when a new election was called.

The NUWSS supported Mr Gulland in the by-election in July 1909, although the WSPU would not support him. Nevertheless, the Liberals held their seat at a reduced majority.

CHAPTER EIGHT

Miscellany

A few abbreviations and what they stood for:

ENSWS (1867-1918)
Edinburgh National Society for Women's Suffrage was the first society in Scotland for women's suffrage (Lydia Becker assembled the English branch in January of that year). Agnes McLaren and Eliza Wigham were joint secretaries. Priscilla McLaren (stepmother to Agnes) was president.

WLF (1887-1988)
Women's Liberal Federation commenced in England in 1887 under the leadership of Catherine Gladstone. The Scottish branch was formed in 1892, with Ishbel Hamilton-Gordon (Lady Aberdeen) as president. One of their objectives was 'to secure just and equal legislation and representation for women and the removal of all legal disabilities on account of sex'.

ILP (1893-1975)
Independent Labour Party commenced in 1893 and both male and females were involved. It was formed by

THE LATE MISS LYDIA BECKER.
(From a Photograph by Warwick Brookes.)

Lydia Becker. (Courtesy of LSE Library)

Scotsman Keir Hardie. For the most part it encouraged women in politics. The **Women's Labour League** was an affiliated group of the ILP, for women. The Glasgow branch commenced in 1908.

WSPU (1903-1917)

Women's Social and Political Union was formed by Emmeline Pankhurst and daughters Christabel and Sylvia. The former two women were the group leaders. The members who started the group had been part of the NUWSS but were unhappy with the protests and lobbying of the former non-militant group. WSPU was a female

Flora Drummond
WSPU
(pictured under
banner) with
suffragettes.
(Courtesy of
LSE Libary)

militant organisation only. They wanted sexual equality and a right to women's votes. Their motto was, 'Deeds not Words'. They were called suffragettes.

NUWSS (1897-1919) (then changed its name)
National Union of Women's Suffrage Societies was formed in 1897 by British woman Millicent Fawcett who wanted enfranchisement for women, but the group did so by non-militant methods. They were called suffragists. There were nearly 500 local, regional and affiliated NUWSS groups throughout the UK. The Scottish section was called the **Scottish Federation of Women's Suffrage Societies.** The idea was decided in the summer of 1909, and November saw the first of its meetings in Edinburgh. Miss S.E.S. Mair was the president and Doctor Elsie Inglis was the secretary.

WFL (1907-1961)
Women's Freedom League was established in 1907 by English suffragettes Charlotte Despard, Teresa Billington-Greig, Alice Schofield, Edith How-Martin and Margaret Nevison. They left WSPU due to a disagreement with Christabel Pankhurst. The League commenced with seventy members who preferred non-violent actions, but kept up the protest. In 1914 there were eleven branches in Scotland. It was originally called the **National Women's Social and Political Union.**

NMF (1913-1918)
Northern Men's Federation supported the women's cause for suffrage. John Wilson McLaren wrote a verse to highlight the journey to Westminster from Scotland: 'We've come from the North, and the heather's on fire, to fight for the women our only desire' were the first few words that say it all.

PL (1884-2004)
Primrose League was a conservative group of female conservatives who were often part of the Ladies Grand Council. Julia, Marchioness of Tweeddale (borders of south-east Scotland) was part of this

group. It has been argued that this group was non-committal about women's suffrage, but they did join in the peaceful march in October 1907 in Edinburgh.

This is just a sample of suffrage organisations. There were many more, including temperance societies, actresses' suffrage, writers' suffrage, and many local area groups of the branches above that sprung up around Scotland, as well as the anti-suffrage groups and other men's groups that supported suffrage. For the purpose of this book they cannot all be recorded, but it is worth delving into the history behind some of them.

Some publications associated with suffrage

Women's Suffrage Journal (1870-1890)

English woman Lydia Becker, who was president of the Manchester Women's Suffrage Society, founded this magazine with Jessie Boucherett. The publication carried a piece in 1872 about Scotland allowing women to vote on school boards (as they did in England).

Votes for Women (1907-1912)

A publication by WSPU, published in October 1907 by Emmeline & Frederick Pethick-Lawrence. A monthly newspaper for six months, and then printed fortnightly. At its height, 30,000 copies were circulated. Due to militant action by WSPU, the Pethick-Lawrences were arrested and imprisoned. They were against the militancy and were expelled, and the newspaper ceased.

The Suffragette (1912-1915)

Was established by WSPU after the above newspaper folded. Christabel Pankhurst took up editorship. The government tried to suppress it, but its 17,000 copies circulation was never as great as *Votes for Women*.

The Britannia (1915-1918)

Another publication edited by Christabel during the war years. Emmeline Pankhurst, Anne Kenney and Scotswoman Flora

Drummond were all part of this newspaper. It was supposed to be patriotic, as the suffrage cause was suspended during the war. However, it appears Christabel often attacked officials in the publication for not being more robust in the war effort.

The Women's Dreadnought (1914-1924)
Sylvia Pankhurst started up the East London Federation of Suffragettes, and this was their official publication. In 1914, the name was changed to The Workers' Suffrage Federation, and the publication name became the *Workers' Dreadnought.* It was no longer associated with WSPU.

The Common Cause (1909-1920)
This was the newspaper of the NUWSS group. Helena Swanwick was an English suffragist who became the first editor. There appears to have been some clashes in the publication with WSPU.

The Vote (1909-1933)
This was the publication of the Women's Freedom League, headed by English suffragist Charlotte Despard. Their members were the writers of the newspaper.

Women's Suffrage Record (1903-1906)
According to the British Newspaper Archive, this publication was by an unknown publisher. It was printed quarterly and reported on various suffrage groups around the country, parliamentary discussions and general pieces on women's unselfishness.

Men/politicians relevant to suffragette cause and why

William Ewart Gladstone (1809-1898)
Born to Scottish parents, Liberal prime minister from 1868-1894 on four separate occasions. When John Stuart Mill proposed amendments to the Reform Bill in 1867, to allow rights for women, Gladstone opposed this, and it was defeated in parliament. In 1884,

the third reform bill amendment for women to obtain the vote was defeated due to Gladstone opposing it. He felt if women got the vote, they would go down the Conservative route.

3rd **Marquess of Salisbury** (1830-1903)

Robert Gascoyne-Cecil, Marquess of Salisbury, was Conservative prime minister three times over a period of thirteen years between 1885 and 1902. Although Gladstone's Reform Bill 1884 did not grant women the vote, the marquess told MP John Manners' wife that he did not regard women's suffrage as high priority, but if ploughmen are capable, then why not educated women?

Arthur Balfour (1848-1930)

He was nephew to the 3rd Marquess above. He was born in Lothian, Scotland, and became Conservative prime minister from 1902-1905. His Liberal sisters-in-law Frances and Betty Balfour tried to engage him in women's enfranchisement, but it was said although he sympathised, due to his party being unreceptive to women's votes nothing was achieved.

Henry Campbell-Bannerman (1836-1908)

Born in Glasgow, Henry served as prime minister from 1905-1908. He did support suffrage. In May 1906, he reportedly said on the cause by the women: 'They made a conclusive and irrefutable case.' However, he appeared to do nothing about the situation and told the women to 'go on pestering, and exercise virtue of patience'. This, of course, infuriated many women committed to the cause.

Herbert Henry Asquith (1852-1928)

Became Liberal prime minister from 1908-1916. He was very much against women's suffrage, even in the late 1800s. Asquith's constituency in 1886 was in fact East Fife. He was targeted many times by the suffragettes, due to his opposition to the cause. He declared in 1913 that 'No other suffrage bill would be considered for an indeterminate time'.

David Lloyd George (1863-1945)
Succeeded Asquith from 1916-1922 as Liberal prime minister. It appears he was very 'hot and cold' regarding women's suffrage. As an MP, he claimed his support for votes for women, but Christabel Pankhurst believed he was actually anti-suffrage. In 1913, a house that was being built for him was fire-bombed by the suffragettes. However, during his time in office, in 1918, the Representation of the People Act gave women over 30 the vote. This was a coalition government.

Andrew Bonar Law (1858-1923)
Conservative Bonar Law was only prime minister for a year, 1922-23, due to illness. He was believed to have been a supporter of women's suffrage, although he apparently said of the cause: 'The less part we take in this discussion the better.' Born in Canada, he lived from 1870 in Helensburgh, Scotland.

Stanley Baldwin (1867-1947)
The Conservative MP became prime minister three times between 1923 and 1937. It was 1928 that saw his government grant adult suffrage to male and females over 21. According to parliament he said: 'I used to vote against women's suffrage. I was taught by the war, which taught me many things.'

Neville Chamberlain (1869-1940)
Prime minster from 1937-1940, he was primarily associated with his appeasement foreign policy prior to the Second World War. However, a recent article in the *Spectator* records that Neville was against women's suffrage prior to the 1918 and 1928 Acts. His half-sister Beatrice was previously anti-suffrage, then apparently became more involved in women's rights, after the vote was given to women, according to her obituary in *The Times*.

Winston Churchill (1874-1965)
Became Conservative prime minster from 1940-1945 and 1951-1955. Earlier in his political career he was opposed to women's suffrage as he felt women were represented by fathers, brothers and

husbands, although this comment was recently challenged by an American historian. When the vote was given in 1928 to women over 21 he, like many Conservative politicians, feared women would then vote for the other parties in an election. His wife Clementine was originally a Liberal and supporter of votes for women.

Lord Curzon (1859-1925)
Was a Conservative politician and in 1912 became the leader of The National League for Opposing Women's Suffrage. A leaflet published after 1910 contained *15 Good Reasons Against the Grant of Female Suffrage*. In 1912, he attended Glasgow at the Scottish Anti-Suffrage League addressing each of these reasons.

John Stuart Mill (1806-1873)
Liberal MP born in England, the first parliamentary member to call for women's suffrage. In 1866, he presented parliament with a petition from women calling for their enfranchisement. This was never achieved in his lifetime, but did it help give the women recognition?

Duncan McLaren (1800-1886)
Was a Liberal MP for Edinburgh in 1865 and, by then, married to Priscilla (Bright), who was the first president of the Edinburgh National Society for Women's Suffrage. He held the first public meeting in 1870 in Edinburgh with his wife's Liberal MP brother, Jacob Bright, in favour of women's suffrage. Another meeting was held in 1871. Another Liberal MP brother John Bright supported universal suffrage.

Keir Hardie (1856-1915)
Scottish politician and leader of the Labour Party from 1906-1908, Keir was a strong supporter of women's votes. He gave his support to WSPU, despite causing rifts in his party. He did not agree with the way suffragettes were treated in prison and frequently protested on this matter.

Richard Haldane (1805-1877)
A Liberal MP born in Edinburgh, in 1885 he represented a Scottish seat in parliament for East Lothian. It is reported he supported female

suffrage, but in Christabel Pankhurst's biography by June Purvis, as a child Christabel listened to conversations of her parents' about Haldane's promising but not delivering. He had said he would back her father's draft of the Women's Disabilities Removal Bill, which included married women's suffrage, but did in fact not bring it to vote. He claimed it 'was a declaration of principle', but it seems he did not truly believe it would come to fruition.

Ramsay Macdonald (1866-1937)
Born in Lossiemouth, Morayshire, Ramsay became Labour prime minister in 1924 and then 1929-1935 (in between Baldwin's stints). He was a supporter of women's suffrage, stating: 'It was a necessary part of a socialist programme.' In 1928, when votes for over-21s came into force, he said: 'We have had our differences, but never had differenced about women's franchise. As for the great body of people in this country is concerned, the victory was won before a shot fired in the European war.'

Monarchs' relevant reigns

Queen Victoria (1819-1901) reigned from 1837-1901
Edward VII (1841-1910) reigned from 1901-1910
George V (1865-1936) reigned from 1910-1936
George VI (1895-1952) reigned from 1936-1952

Quotes from distinguished figures of the time

Winston Churchill (1908): 'Nothing would induce me to give women the franchise.'

Winston Churchill (post First World War): 'Women ought not to be treated as men, the sooner they are back in their homes the better.'

Charles Darwin: 'Equality is scientifically impossible. Men are clever, because over the millennia their brains have become honed by chasing animals and defending the family. Lesser female brain power is an inescapable consequence of nature.' (From his book *The Descent of a Man, and Selection in Relation to Sex*.)

Francis Galton (Darwin's cousin): 'It was the duty of intelligent girls to rear clever boys and domesticated daughters, and not to indulge themselves by studying science or earning money!'

William Knight (Professor of Philosophy): 'To grant parliamentary vote to women would be a burden to inflict on them, a burden too grievous to bear'.(*Anti-Suffrage Review* 4/5/1911.)

John Stuart Mill (MP in favour of Suffrage): 'Inequality of women was a relic from the past, when might was right'. (From his book *The Subjection of Women 1869 - Equality Between Sexes*.)

Queen Victoria (opposed to suffrage): 'If women were to unsex themselves by claiming equality with men, they would become the most hateful, heathen and disgusting beings, and would surely perish without male protection.' (Comments made by the queen in 1870.)

Sir Almoth Wright (bacteriologist): 'They [the suffragettes] are sexually embittered women in whom everything has turned to gall and bitterness and hatred of men.' (From his book *The Unexpurgated Case against Women's Suffrage*')

Keir Hardie (Scottish politician): 'No one seeks to deny the existences of differences between the sexes, but man does not have the right to say what duties and responsibilities women must undertake, and what must be withheld because of her sex.' (From his book *The Citizenship of Women: A Plea for Women's Suffrage*.)

Again, so many men and women were involved over the years for and against women's enfranchisement, and apologies for not being able to comment on all concerned.

Conclusion

A thirst for historical knowledge and the challenge to research Scottish suffrage was the basis for writing this book. Although not a historian, as a published writer of various articles and previous journalistic experience it was my aim to collect information and images on suffrage and personal accounts from relatives of suffragettes/suffragists. Gathering essential information about working lives, education, health and welfare of Scotland's women as a whole was invaluable in building the profile of women's right to vote.

Indirectly, the path that lay before these women in history was just as important as the few years prior to the 1918 enfranchisement of women over 30, and then onwards to 1928 and the vote for women aged 21 and over.

The book is not meant to be judgemental but to give fair and accurate (so far as research allows) accounts of the final result of women's enfranchisement.

Were the suffragettes too militant? Would women have achieved the vote if nothing had been done all those years ago? Could the suffragists with their non-militant campaign have won we women the vote? Lots of questions and everyone has their own answers. Many historians over the years have debated why women didn't get the vote originally, and of course only certain men could vote to begin with, but over the years it has all changed.

Politicians from various parties often felt if they gave enfranchisement to women, they would lose political advantage.

Some historians felt the suffragettes that kept up the militancy, rightly or wrongly, gave it precedence in the news in a great deal of publications for the suffrage cause. The fact they were willing to put their lives in danger to achieve a political voice for women, to some, spoke volumes.

It has also been quoted from other historians that the war gave women enfranchisement due to their hard and varied war effort work, so women aged 30 were repaid by being allowed to vote in 1918. However, in reply to this, others have said it was also young women under 30 who helped in the war, working in munitions factories, carrying out work in the service industries such as postal workers, the police, and various other forms of work. These women were denied the vote at that time. Did the militancy of the suffragettes divert attention away from the actual cause? Didn't the government then not want to give in to criminal activity, hence imprisonment when suffragettes failed to pay their fines? Force-feeding women during their protest hunger strikes does not sit well with many people, whatever their views. Many women were physically and mentally scarred for the rest of their lives. This was due to the rough handling of the gastric tubing, which appears not always to have been delivered to the stomach via the oesophagus but inadvertently inserted into the lungs, causing pneumonia and respiratory problems, not to mention the tearing of the oesophagus lining as the tube was abrasively inserted. So again, there are arguments for both sides and, of course, everyone has an opinion.

My aim in collating the material for this book was to be impartial and allow the reader to absorb the information and varied pictures in a fairly easy-to-read style that young and old alike could understand.

Whatever your views and opinions on women's enfranchisement, it was a matter in history for a good number of years. It did not fade into the background, it made headlines, good or bad, depending on your thoughts, but in the end the women won the right to vote, first in 1918 for females over 30, for over 21s (male and female) in 1928, and then for all voters aged 18 in 1970. Scotland's Independent Referendum Act 2013 gave the vote to 16-year-old male and female constituents in Scotland just for that particular referendum.

So, with all the controversial ups and downs, violence, force-feeding, speeches, parliamentary debates, the voices of the anti-suffrage campaigners, and the gusto of the women suffragettes and suffragists, all was achieved eventually in obtaining votes for women in Scotland, and the UK generally.

In 2018, the centenary year of enfranchisement for women, thousands of females and some men walked in London in the March sunshine. The theme was Gender Equality.

Helen Pankhurst, great-granddaughter of Emmeline Pankhurst and granddaughter of Sylvia Pankhurst, said at the International Women's Day Rally in London: 'Getting the vote didn't resolve everything ... that is why we are here today.' The equality fight still goes on.

In the words of Scottish suffragette Helen Crawfurd, 'Shall we remain silent any longer?'

Bibliography

Books

Abram L., Gordon E., Simonton D., Yeo E. J. *Gender in Scottish History Since 1700* (Edinburgh University Press 2006)

Blair, Catherine *Rural Journey A History of the S.W.R.I, 1917-1939* (Lothian Print 1940)

Bremner D. *Industries of Scotland, Their Rise, Progress, & Present Condition.* 1869 (New York – A.M. Kelly 1969)

Brientenback E.R. *Scottish Women: A Documentary History 1780-1914* (Edinburgh University Press 2013)

Carolan, Janet *Lavina Malcom - First Woman Town Councillor & Provost* (Journal 2007) accessed 2018

Christie, Thomas A., Lovett, Margaret L. *A Cloud of Witnesses From Saints to Suffragettes Around Stirling* (Robert Greene 2011)

Cooke, Anthony *History of Drinking* (Edinburgh University 2015)

Crawford E. *The Women's Suffrage Movement: 1866-1928* (Routledge 1998)

Edwards, Elaine *Scotland's Land Girls – Breeches, Bombers & Backaches* (NSME 2010)

Ewan E., Evan L., Innes S., Phillips S., Piper R. *Biographical Dictionary of Scottish Women,*(Edinburgh University Press 2013 – 2012)

Fraser H.W., Lee C.H. *Aberdeen 1800-2000, A New History* (Tuckwell Press 2000)

Garrower-Gray A. *Scotland's Hidden Harlots & Heroines*, (Pen & Sword 2014)

Girvan, Edith *Changing Life in Scotland & Britain 1830-1930*, (Heinemann 2004)

Gordon E., Nair G. *The Economic Role of Middle Class Women in Victorian Glasgow* (History Review 2007)

Gottilieb V., Toye R. *The Aftermath of Suffrage: Women, Gender & Politics in Britain, 1918-1945* (Palgrave & Macmillan 2013)

Joannou M., Purvis J. *The Women's Suffrage Movement: New Feminist Perspective* (Manchester University Press 1998)

King, Elspeth *Old Stirling* (Stenlake 2009)

King, Elspeth *Stirling Girls* (Smith Art Gallery & Museum 2003)

Knox W.J. *Lives of Scottish Women: 1800-1980* (Edinburgh University Press 2006)

Leneman, Leah *A Guid Cause: The Women's Suffrage Movement in Scotland* (Aberdeen University Press 1991)

Leneman, Leah *The Scottish Suffragettes* (NMS 2000)

Mahood, Linda *The Magadelenes: Prostitution in the 19th Century* (Routledge 2012)

Mambury, Chris *People's History of Scotland* (Verso 2014)

Marlow, Joyce *Suffragettes: The Fight for Votes for Women* (Virago 2015)

McDermid, Jane *The Schooling of Working Class Girls in Victorian Scotland* (Routledge 2005)

Meighan, Michael *Glasgow History* (Amberley 2013)

Miskell L., Whatley C., Harris B. *Victorian Dundee Image, & Realities* (Tuckwell 2000)

Moffat, Alistair *Scotland – A History from Earliest Times* (Birlinn Ltd 2015)

Pederson, Sarah *Caroline Phillips, Suffragette & Journalist* (Robert Gordon University 2017)

Reid, Marion *A Plea for Woman* (William Tait 1843, Polygon 1988)

Rover, Constance *Women's Suffrage – Party Politics in Britain* (Routledge & K Paul 1967)

Settle, Louise *Sex for Sale in Scotland – Prostitution in Glasgow & Edinburgh, 1900-1939* (Edinburgh University Press 2016)

Smith P. *Lord Salisbury on Politics: A Selection from his articles in Quarterly Review* (New York: Cambridge University Press 2008)

Smout, T.C. *A Century of the Scottish People: 1830-1950* (Element 2010)

Stephenson, Jayne *The Home Front: Stirling, 1939-45* (Stirling District Libraries 1991)

Tubbs M., McCaughie J. *Edinburgh Memories* (History Press 2009)

Vellacott J. *From Liberal to Labour with Women's Suffrage: The story of Catherine Marshall* (Spokesman 2016)

Wollstonecraft, Mary *A vindication of the rights of Woman* (Vintage 2015)

Websites

www.bora.vib.no/btstream/handle

www.core.ac.uk/temperancewomensmovement

www.darkdundee.co.uk

www.discoverydundee.ac.uk

www.edinburghmuseums.com/votes For women

www.futuremuseum.co.uk

www.genguide.co.uk

www.geni.com

www.histed.centre.or.uk

www.historylearningsite.co.uk

www.howglasgowflourished.wordpress.com

www.islandbritain.org.uk

www.jamesgillespieprimary.co.uk

www.kosmoid.net

www.localhistories.org

www.lucy

www.maidinperth.org/suffragette-movementinperth

www.nls.uk/displayonwomenscientists

www.ochils.org.uk

www.saltiresociety.org.uk

www.scotsman-com/news/edinburgh-and-sex-city-seedy-history-laid-bare

www.scran.ac.uk/scotland

www.shetlandmuseumsarchives.org

www.silvervault.org.uk

www.spartus-educational.com

www.visitscotland.com

www.welcometolennoxtown.co.uk/history

www.womenforindependence.org

www.womenshistoryscotland.org

Index

Aberdeen Daily Journal;
  Caroline, Phillips,
    Journalist, 72
Aberdeen Female School of
  Industry, 68
Aberdeen Ladies Educational
  Association, 80–1
Aberdeen Ladies Union
  (ABL), 66
Aberdeen Station, 69
Aberdeen Suffrage Society, 71
Aberdeen university, 69
*Address to the women of Great
  Britain* Pamphlet, 1843, 43
Aithrey Spa Bowling Green,
  incident, 99
Allan, Janie, 55
Allt-an-Fhionn property, 39
Anti-Suffrage League, 61,
  99, 134
Ashley Road incident,
  Aberdeen, 70
Asquith, PM Herbert
  Henry, 132
    attacked by Lilias Mitchell at
      Dornoch Golf course, 77
    attacked by various
      suffragettes at
      Bannockburn, 99
    petition in 1909 and Lila
      Clunas, 58

Asylums, 88
Atholl, Duchess of, 24, 61–2

Baird, Lady Matilda, 67
Baldwin, PM Stanley, 133
Balfour, Prime Minister Arthur,
  18, 132
Balfour, Lady Betty, 19
Balfour, Lady Frances, 18
    connection with Whitekirk
      Church, 19
    spoke in the Highlands and
      Islands, 112
Balmoral Golf course, 77
Bank of Scotland, 2
    women to resign when
      married, 2
Barlow, Annie, 96
Beaston, Sir George;
    confrontation with Elsie
      Inglis, 18
Becker, Lydia, 127
    founded *Women's Suffrage
      Journal* in 1870, 130
Begg, Faithful, xv
Bennett, Dr Henry;
    comment on females to train
      as doctors, 15
Bevan, MP Aneurin, 70
Billington-Greig,
    Teresa, 73–4

Blair, Catherine
    Edinburgh, 11–13
Bright, Jacob, brother to
    Priscilla Mclaren, 25, 91
Bright, Prime Minister John, 22
Britannia, The, 130
British Woman's Temperance
    Association, 94
Brothels in 1800's, 5
Brown, Nannie (Agnes), 13
Brown, Jessie, 13

Calton Jail, Edinburgh;
    force feeding of Ethel
        Moorhead, 53
Campbell-Bannerman,
    Sir Henry MP, 97–8, 132
Carrie, Isabella, 55
Cat & Mouse Act, 1913, xii, 40
    Ethel Moorhead released, 53
Catholic Women's Society for
    Suffrage, 23
Caudron aircraft factory,
    Alloa, 86–7
Chalmers-Smith, Dr Elizabeth
    Dorothea, 40
Chamberlain, PM Neville, 133
Christison, Professor Robert;
    comment on females to train
        as doctors, 15
Churchill, PM Winston, 133–5
    egg thrown at him by Ethel
        Moorhead, 52
    Isabella Carrie manhandled, 55
    Lila Clunas thrown out of
        Dundee Meeting in 1908, 57
    opposed to women's Vote, 58

Clunas, Lila, 57
Common Cause, newspaper of
    NUWSS, 131
Conciliation Bills, 98
Conolan, Miss G., 98
Contagious Diseases
    Act, 23–4
Craig, Anna Rhoda, 39-40, 97
    see also Robinson (Craig),
        Rhoda
Craigen, Jessie;
    meeting at Stenhousemuir,
        Stirling, 92
    spoke in Highlands, 112
Cranston, Miss Kate, 31
Crawfurd, Helen, 38–9, 139
Crichton, Elizabeth, 121
Crudelius, Mary, 20–1
Curzon, Lord, 134

'Deeds not Words', 128
Dixie, Lady Florence, 123–4
Domestic & Textile
    Industries & women, 3
Dornoch Golf course, 77
Drummond, Flora, 107–108
Drummond, Victoria,
    goddaughter to Queen
        Victoria, 62
Dudhope castle, Dundee, 52
Dundee;
    Farrington Hall, 52
    first Scottish city to imprison
        Women, 52
Dundee Advertiser, 52
Dundee and District Domestic
    Servants Association, 48

Dundee and District Rescue
Home for Fallen Women, 50

Edinburgh Conservative and
Unionist Women's Franchise
Association, 19
Edinburgh Education, 7, 35
dame schools, 51
for aristocratic girls, 8
Mrs Black Glasgow
commenced evening
classes for girls, 120
Edinburgh Emancipation
Society, 9
Edinburgh Evening Dispatch
article, 55
Edinburgh Female Anti-Slavery
Society, 9
Edinburgh Hospital and
Dispensary for Women and
Children, 19
Edinburgh Ladies Education
Association (ELEA), 20
Edinburgh March 1909, 107
Edinburgh National Society for
Women's Suffrage, 21, 23,
91, 127
Edinburgh National Women's
Suffrage 1886, 10
Edinburgh School of Medicine
for Women (ESMW), 15
Edinburgh Seven, 14
Edinburgh Society for Women's
Suffrage (ESWS), 22
Agnes Mclaren, 24
Education (Scotland) Act 1872,
7, 35, 51, 68, 105–106, 120

Edinburgh University, 2,
14–15, 21
Edinburgh Women's March
1912, 13
Elder, Isabella, 35–6
Esslemont, Dr Mary, 70–1
Medical Degree 1923, 68
National Women's Federation
and NHS, 70

Fairlie, Margaret, 51
Female journalists, 45
Women's World, 46
Fergusson, Christian Jane, 126
Ferguson-Watson, Dr Hugh,
43, 53
First Female football team;
see Mathews (Graham),
Helen
First World War, xi, 2–3, 12,
17, 21, 39, 51, 57, 89, 103,
108, 111, 118
aircraft factory, 85–6
government munitions
factory, Gretna, 118
Forward newspaper;
Grieson, Jane, 94
Fraser, Helen, 69, 112

Garrett Anderson, Elizabeth, 16
Garrett Anderson, Dr Louisa, 122
Garrett Fawcett, Millicent,
101–102, 129
Gilchrist, Dr Marion, 35, 40–1
Gladstone, William, 131–2
1884 Third Reform Act, 9–10
Glasgow subway, 33

Glasgow and West Scotland
    Association for Women's
    Suffrage, 41
*Gloriana, or the Revolution of
    1900,* a book on women with
    votes 1890, 123–4
Gorbals Female Universal
    Suffrage Society, 42
Gordon, Frances, 43
Govan trained nurses, 105
Grant, May Pollock;
    see Marion Pollock, 71
Grieson, Jane, 94
Gulland, John William, MP for
    Dumfries, 126

Haldane, MP Richard, 134–5
Hamilton-Gordon, Ishbel
    (Marchioness of Aberdeen),
    75–6, 127
Hardie, Keir, xiv–xv, 107,
    134, 136
    first leader of ILP, 44, 128
Harvard Medical School, 15
Hay Abbot, Wilhemina, 112
Hazelbank house, 115
Highlands & Islands Medical
    Services, 6, 24, 105
Highland Times, 115
Holme, Vera (Jack), 124–5
Holyrood Palace, 2, 4
Horsburgh, Florence, 58–60
Howie, Elsie, 114

Independent Labour Party,
    107, 127
    Helen Crawfurd becomes a
    member, 39

Jessie Stephens organises
    maidservants, 42
*Industrial and Social Position
    of Women,* 81
Inglis, Dr Elsie Maud, 16,
    124, 129
    speaks in the Highlands and
    Islands, 112
Institute of Marine Engineers;
    first female member, Victoria
    Drummond, 62
International Council of Women;
    first president, 76

Jamieson, Christina, 108–10
Jamieson, Eveline, 124
Jenners, Edinburgh, 4
Jex-Blake, Dr Sophia, 14–16, 21
    see also Inglis,
        Dr Elsie Maud
        McLaren, Agnes

Kelly, Jane;
    friends with Florence
        Horsburgh, 60
King George V, 52, 55, 62,
    109, 135
Kirkland Reid, Marion, 37–8
    A Plea for a Woman, xv

Ladies Auxiliary Emancipation
    Society in Glasgow, 43
Ladies Emancipation
    Society, 24
Ladies Edinburgh Debating
    Society, 9, 21
    see also Sarah Siddons 21
Ladies National Association, 23

Lennox, Agnes, 42
London Women's Suffrage
    Meeting 1871, 25
Ladies Educational
    Association;
    Aberdeen Branch, 69
Ladies Working Society, 66
Lamond, W.H., 98–9
Leisk, Harriet, 111
Lloyd George, David, 53,
    69, 133
    affray at music hall,
        Aberdeen, 56, 71
    attacked at Albert Hall, 77–8
Lumsden, Louisa Innes, 71
Lytton, Lady Constance, 19

Macdonald, PM Ramsay, 135
Maclean, Elizabeth, 89
Macpherson, Katherine, 62
Macmillan, Chrystal;
    speaker at Bridge of Allan,
        1911, 96
    speech at Hyde Park, 71
    spoke in the Highlands and
        Islands, 1909, 112
Magadalen Ayslum, 5
Mair, Sarah Elizabeth Siddons,
    21–2, 129
Malcolm, Lavinia, 96–7
Manhood Franchise
    Bill 1912, 98
Marchioness of Tullibardine;
    see Duchess of Atholl
Married Women's Property Act;
    put forward by Duncan &
        Priscilla McClaren, 25
    more rights for females, 32

Masson, Professor David,
    21, 25
Matthews (Graham),
    Helen, 94–5
Mayo, Isabel Fyvie, 79–81
McCallum, Janet (Jenny), 91–2
Mclagan, Christian, 94
McLaren, Agnes, 21, 23–4,
    112, 121
    joint secretary to ENSWS, 127
McLaren, Duncan MP, 22,
    25, 134
McLaren, Priscilla, 22-3, 127
Medical Professional Career
    discrimination, 4
Men's League for Women's
    Suffrage, (MLWS), 44,
    97, 114
Men's Political Union for
    Women's Enfranchisement, 97
*Militant Suffrage Movement
    mention,* by Teresa
    Billington-Greig, 74
Mill, John Stuart MP, 22, 25,
    134, 136
    penned article in support of
        women's Suffrage, 26
Milne, John Duguid, 81
Mitchell, Malcom J., 114
Mitchell, Lilias, 77, 114
Moffatt, Graham, 44
Moffatt, Maggie, 43
Montrose, Duchess of, 99
Moorhead, Ethel, 52–5, 97
    house fire attempt with
        Dr Chalmers- Smith, 40
    Robbie Burns house fire by
        Ethel Moorhead, 56

Murray, Dr Flora, 122–3
Murray, James MP, 81

National Association of
  Training Corps for girls;
  Health Minister Florence
    Horsburgh organises the
    Group, 59
  smashes Wallace
    glass case, 53
National Council for Working
  Women, 18
National Federation of Women
  Workers, 42, 49, 86
National Insurance Act 1911,
  6, 34
National League for Opposing
  Women's Suffrage, 134
National Society for Women's
  Suffrage, 18, 21, 23, 91,
  127, 134
  Jane E. Taylour, honorary
    secretary of Galloway
    branch, 121
National Union of Women's
  Suffrage Society, (NUWSS),
  17, 19, 21, 23–4, 38, 71,
  76, 95, 109, 112, 123, 126,
  128–9, 131
National Union of Women
  Workers, 66
National Women's
  Federation, 70
National Women's Social and
  Political Union (former name
  of WFL), 129

North British Rubber
  Company, 118–19
Northern Men's Association for
  Women's Suffrage 1910, 21
Northern Men's Federation
  (NMF), 97, 129

Ogston, Helen, 77–9
Onwards and Upwards
  Association;
  see Aberdeen, Marchioness of

Paisley Mill, 31
Pankhurst, Adela, 69
  spoke in Highlands
    1909-11, 112
Pankhurst, Christabel;
  comment on Isabel Fvyie
    Mayo, 81
  correspondence with
    Caroline Phillips, 72
  disagreement with women
    who then formed
    WFL, 129
  editorship of *The Britannia*
    publication with
    others, 130–1
  editorship of *The Suffragette*
    publication, 130
  formed the WSPU with her
    mother and Sylvia, 128
  spoke at Aberdeen Meeting
    1908, 69
Pankhurst, Emmeline;
  correspondence with
    Caroline Phillips, 72

formed the WSPU with her
  daughters, 128
spoke in the Highlands,
  1909-11, 112
Pankhurst, Helen, Great-
  granddaughter of
  Emmeline, 139
Pankhurst, Sylvia;
  account of Helen Ogston, 79
  formed the WSPU with
    mother and Christabel, 128
  relationship with Keir
    Hardie, 44
  takes over Aberdeen branch
    from Caroline Phillips, 72
Parker, Fanny, 56
  incident at Aberdeen
    music hall, 71
Penicuik Paper Mill, 3
Perth Prison, 43, 46–7, 53
  Ethel Moorhead, 53, 56
  Fanny Parker, 56
Pethick-Lawrence, Emmeline,
  WSPU publication, 130
Phillips, Caroline, 72–3,
  77, 81
Pollock, Marion, 71
Poorhouses, 6, 24, 34, 50, 88
  Kirkcudbright poorhouse,
    Dumfries, 119
Poor Law (Scotland)
  Act 1845, 104
Primrose League 1883, 129–30
  Edinburgh branch, 10
  Lady Frances Balfour's
    involvement, 18

Prostitution;
  Dundee and District Rescue
    Home for fallen women, 50
  in Aberdeen Industrial
    Reformatory and
    Asylum, 67
  in Glasgow, 33
  in Stirling, 89
Public Baths & Washhouses, 6
Pullar, Mrs Edmund, 95–6
Pullars factory, Perth, 49
Pullinger, Dorothee, 119

Queen's Jubilee nurses, 105
Queen Margaret College,
  Glasgow, 40
Queen Victoria, 62, 136

Ragged Schools, 7–8, 90
Reform Acts 1832, 1867 &
  1884, xi–xv, 9, 88
  proposed amendment To
    1867 by John
    Stuart Mills, 22
Representation of the People's
  Acts, vii, xi–xii, xv, 133
Robinson (Craig),
  Rhoda, 39–40
Rose, Dr Elizabeth, 90

Salisbury, 3rd Marquess, 132
Saxby, Jessie, 110
Scott-Murray, Margaret, 61
Scotsman, The, 121
  advert for females to train as
    doctors, 14

comment on Lady Frances
  Balfour, 18
report of Farrington Hall
  arson, 52
Scottish and English Women's
  Liberal Federation, 126
Scottish Association for the
  Medical Education of
  Women (SAMED), 16
Scottish Churches League for
  Women's Suffrage, 19, 71
Scottish Convention of Women
  (SCOW) 71
Scottish Co-operative Women's
  Guild, 93
Scottish Council of Women's
  Citizens Association, 13
Scottish Domestic Workers
  Union, 42
Scottish Federation of
  Women's Suffrage Societies,
  16, 112, 129
Scottish Unionist Party;
  Duchess of Atholl, 25
Scottish Universities Women's
  Suffrage Union, 56
Scottish Women's Hospitals,
  (SWH), 17, 124
Scottish Women's Rural
  Institute, 11, 13
Scrymgeour, Edwin MP, 58
Shetland Suffrage
  Society, 109–10
  chairwoman Harriet
    Leisk, 111
  write about Cathcart
    Wasson, MP, 114

Sketch of votes for women's
  movement, 109
Smeal, Jane, 42–3
Smeal Wigham, Eliza, 9
Society for Equal
  Citizenship, 21
Snowden, Ethel, 110
St Andrews University,
  26, 48, 77
St Mungo patron saint of
  Glasgow, 29
Stephens, Jessie, 42
Stirling Female Society for the
  Relief of Aged and Indigent
  Women, 89
Stirling Observer, 99
Stirling Women's Unionist
  Association, 96
Suffragette Publication, 130
  Ashley Road incident,
    Aberdeen, 70
  copy sent to police on
    Farrington Hall incident, 52
Suffragettes, 11–13, 18–20,
  26–8, 36, 42–4, 46–7, 52–3,
  55–6, 58, 60–2, 69–70, 72–3,
  77–9, 92–4, 97, 99, 108, 110,
  114–16, 122–4, 126,
  128–34, 136–9
  term from Daily Mail
    reporter, 98

Taylour, Jane, 91–2, 112, 121–2
Teaching, 3, 7–9,
  pay difference between
    sexes, 91, 121
Temperance Act 1913, 89

Templeton Carpet factory, 31
The Education Act 1918, 8
The National Health Service, 6

Vote 100 Project 2018, xvi
Vote The WFL, publication, 131
    Fanny Parker wrote report on
        her time in Perth prison, 56
    Keir Hardie writes for
        publication, 44

Wallace monument incident;
    see Ethel Moorhead, 97
Wallace-Dunlop, Marion, 111
Walton, Olive Dundee, 55
Watson, Bessie, 26
Whitekirk Church, 19
Wigham, Eliza, 9, 23–4
    joint secretary to ENSWS, 127
Wollstonecraft, Mary, 91
    Vindication of the Rights of
        Woman, 91
Workers' Dreadnought;
    see Women's
        Dreadnought, 131
Women's Army Auxiliary
    Corps, 57
Women's Conference for
    Peace, 13
Women's Disabilities Removal
    Bill, 135
Women's Dreadnought,
    publication, 131
Women's Freedom League
    (WFL), 13, 72, 93, 129
    convenor and secretary,
        Katherine Macpherson, 62

Janet (Jenny) McCallum,
    imprisoned for rioting, 92
Lila Clunas joins as
    Secretary, 57
see also Maggie Moffatt, 43
Women's Freedom League
    National Service
    Organisation, 55
Women's Guild of
    the Empire, 108
Women's Hospital for Children
    in London, 122
Women's Labour League, 128
Women's Liberal Association
    (WLA), 69
Women's Liberal
    Federation, 126–7
    Ishbel Hamilton-Gordon,
        Countess of Aberdeen,
        presidency, 76
Women's Liberal Unionist
    Association (WLUA), 18
Women's Peace Crusade
    (WPC), 39
Women's Police Volunteers;
    Olive Walton, one of four
        female Inspectors, 56
Women's Royal Naval
    Service(WRNS), 103
Women's Social and Political
    Union(WSPU), 128
    Aberdeen WSPU and
        Caroline Phillips, 72
    Dr Elizabeth Chalmers-
        Smith receives Medal, 40
    Helen Crawfurd switches
        from NUWSS, 38

Dr Marion Gilchrist joins
    1907, 41
Fanny Parker, joins is
    arrested, and sent to
    Holloway, 56
Flora Murray sets up
    nursing home for injured
    suffragettes, 122
Jessie Stephens letterbox
    acid for WSPU, 42
Jessie Yuille Stirling leader
    1905, 94
Lila Clunas and sisters join, 57
Maggie Moffatt march into
    London, 43
Scottish council of the
    WSPU and Teresa
    Billington-Greig, 73
Women's Suffrage Journal, 130
Women's Suffrage Record,
    reported on various suffrage
    groups, 131
    on Primrose League, 10
Women's workforce 1800's and
    onwards;
    Broadfield Mill female
        workers strike, 1834, 65
    Calton weavers male workers
        felt threatened by women
        workers, 30

crofting work for females in
    Highlands, 101–102
fishing industry and female
    work Aberdeen, 65
Glasgow Subway women
    workers, 33
Hosiery, Knitting and Carpet
    manufacture for women in
    Dumfries, 117–18
Howietoun fishery female
    workforce, 84
Scottish mining;
    Stirling female work
        workforce, 83–4
Spinning and Weaving in
    Clackmannan, 83
Textile workforce
    in Dundee, 47
    including health
        issues, 50
Whaling industry work
    for women in
    Dundee, 48
woollen mill workers and
    cottars, Aberdeen, 64
    Mary Lilly Walker, helped
        women and children in
        work, 51

Yuille, Jessie, 94